# Fresh Start Bankruptcy

# Fresh Start Bankruptcy

## A Simplified Guide for Individuals and Entrepreneurs

Deborah Levine Herman, Esq.
Robin L. Bodiford, Esq.

**WILEY**

John Wiley & Sons, Inc.

Published by John Wiley & Sons, Inc., Hoboken, New Jersey.
Published simultaneously in Canada.

No part of this publication may be reproduced, stored in a retrieval system, or transmitted in any form or by any means, electronic, mechanical, photocopying, recording, scanning, or otherwise, except as permitted under Section 107 or 108 of the 1976 United States Copyright Act, without either the prior written permission of the Publisher, or authorization through payment of the appropriate per-copy fee to the Copyright Clearance Center, Inc., 222 Rosewood Drive, Danvers, MA 01923, (978) 750-8400, fax (978) 750-4470, or on the web at www.copyright.com. Requests to the Publisher for permission should be addressed to the Permissions Department, John Wiley & Sons, Inc., 111 River Street, Hoboken, NJ 07030, (201) 748-6011, fax (201) 748-6008, e-mail: permcoordinator@wiley.com.

Limit of Liability/Disclaimer of Warranty: While the publisher and author have used their best efforts in preparing this book, they make no representations or warranties with respect to the accuracy or completeness of the contents of this book and specifically disclaim any implied warranties of merchantability or fitness for a particular purpose. No warranty may be created or extended by sales representatives or written sales materials. The advice and strategies contained herein may not be suitable for your situation. The publisher is not engaged in rendering professional services, and you should consult a professional where appropriate. Neither the publisher nor author shall be liable for any loss of profit or any other commercial damages, including but not limited to special, incidental, consequential, or other damages.

For general information on our other products and services please contact our Customer Care Department within the United States at (800) 762-2974, outside the United States at (317) 572-3993 or fax (317) 572-4002.

Wiley also publishes its books in a variety of electronic formats. Some content that appears in print may not be available in electronic books. For more information about Wiley products, visit our web site at www.wiley.com.

This product is not a substitute for legal advice.

*Disclaimer required by Texas Statutes*

This publication is designed to provide accurate and authoritative information in regard to the subject matter covered. It is sold with the understanding that the publisher is not engaged in rendering legal, accounting, or other professional service. If legal or other expert assistance is required, the services of a competent professional person should be sought.

*From a Declaration of Principles Jointly Adopted by a Committee of the American Bar Association and a Committee of Publishers and Associations*

How to use a self-help law book: It is your responsibility to make sure that the facts and general advice contained in this book applies to your situation. We have made every effort to give you the most accurate and up to date information available in this book. But, the laws are always changing and are frequently subject to various interpretations. Seek legal advice if you want legal assistance backed by a guarantee.

*Library of Congress Cataloging-in-Publication Data:*

Herman, Deborah Levine
  Fresh start bankruptcy : a simplified guide for individuals and entrepreneurs / Deborah Levine Herman and Robin L. Bodiford
    p. cm.
  Includes index.
  ISBN 0-471-26313-3 (pbk. : alk. paper)
  1. Bankruptcy—United States—Popular works.  I. Title.
  KF1524.6.H47    2003
  346.7307'8—dc21
                                                                              2002038035

Printed in the United States of America.

10  9  8  7  6  5  4  3  2  1

*To all those who need a fresh start. Don't look back.*

# ACKNOWLEDGMENTS

I would particularly like to thank Robin Bodiford for her significant work in supporting this book with up-to-date substance. Although esquire follows my name, my passion is to explain the practice of law to you—those who need it—in a way that you can understand. If I have been able to remove some of the mystique and enable you to feel less intimidated by the process, I have been successful. Robin is in the trenches on a daily basis as are many fine bankruptcy experts. My goal is to provide you with language and information to wade through the experience with empowerment. Robin supported the project by making sure the law is up-to-date and correct. Although nothing is perfect, I am grateful to Robin for doing all she could to see that errors were not made. Robin was also tireless in helping me to maneuver through the morass of what promises to become universal bankruptcy reform in this country in the near future. If our explanation seems complicated, you should have seen it before Robin dove in head first.

Suzanne Caplan, a wonderful consultant from Pittsburgh, Pennsylvania, added exceptional insights regarding businesses and the implications of bankruptcy. Suzanne also has a thriving practice and guides businesses through economic crises with the finesse of a diplomat and the skill of an artist.

Toni Robino is a miracle and angel in my life. I can always count on Toni to be there whenever I need her in our writing or in our lives. It is truly a blessing to have a colleague and friend who is also a sister of the heart. Her help in the final stages of pulling things together was a Godsend.

I must thank my patient and supportive family. My husband, Jeff Herman, who has traveled with me through all of my detours, and my loving and patient children, Joshua and Jessica, who didn't always whine when I told them, "I can't talk now, I'm writing!" My eldest daughter Shana, who is an inspiration, keeps me focused on my goals.

Last, but not least by any means, I would like to acknowledge my saint of an editor at John Wiley, Mike Hamilton, for his guidance, patience, and support. There are always many other people whose hard work contributes to the ultimate production of a book. They include Linda Indig, my production manager at Wiley, the production staff at Publications Development Company, and those many managers in sales. Although typically behind the scenes, these professionals are the lifeblood of any publishing house. Thank you.

D. L. H.

# CONTENTS

# Fresh Start Bankruptcy

# 1

# Deciding to File

The decision to file bankruptcy is difficult. It has ramifications that are far reaching and life changing. However, remaining in the throes of financial chaos is far worse than finding a tangible and meaningful solution that can bring you back to the stability of financial health.

Bankruptcy filings are at an all-time high of 1.5 million per year. After the tragedy of September 11, 2001, and during these times of financial upheaval in our country, many people found themselves in untenable financial circumstances. If you find yourself in this group, the most important thing to consider is no matter how you have gotten here—lack of money management, over spending, job loss, medical bills, or unexpected changes in your life—your focus needs to be on solutions.

The biggest problem you face as a person considering bankruptcy is your loss of self-esteem. If you are caught up in the idea that bankruptcy should be faced with shame and stigma, you will find the bankruptcy process awful. You are also experiencing fear and anxiety. Remember, you are far from the only one in the world who is in this situation. Bankruptcies are almost epidemic because of the changing climate of our economy and the ridiculously easy access to credit we all have.

As you will see in Chapter 2 in greater detail, we are a country out of control. Most of us have no idea how to use credit. Credit is funny money, but after a while, it becomes necessary to fund the lifestyles to which we have become accustomed.

Although statistics vary, it is estimated that the average family has about $8,500 in credit card debt. This is outrageous. Most bankruptcies are filed because the debtor, you, is no longer able to handle the minimum payments of the many credit accounts you have at any given time.

If you want to make it through the process of bankruptcy without experiencing total trauma and misery, you are going to have to develop a thick skin, objectivity, and the ability to accept your circumstances without the recriminating "what ifs." If you can do these things, you can avoid *decision paralysis.* Once you make the decision to file bankruptcy, the process is essentially black and white. You are the additional ingredient that will determine the quality of the outcome and how well you are able to rebuild your life.

## FACE YOUR SITUATION HEAD-ON

If you are ready to face your situation head-on, you will find that the process of bankruptcy, although it involves material loss, will be the most freeing experience you will probably ever have. If you have been choking in a sea of debt, you are already in the depths of financial despair. Anyone who has experienced a nosedive in income is familiar with humiliation, creditor harassment, uncertainty, and fear. Most of us live in denial of how out of control our financial situation really is. As we see the downward slide, we pretend it isn't happening by filling our desk drawers with unopened bills we know we cannot pay. We find many ways to avoid the truth.

Now that you are looking at the reality of your circumstances, the worst is really over. It may not seem that way at first, but when you unravel your debts and figure out a way toward a fresh start, you will be able to exhale and untie the knots that are permanent residents of your lower intestines. We are not advocating that bankruptcy is your *solution.* By looking directly at your particular money monsters, you will find that there are things you can do before bankruptcy becomes the inevitable next step.

There are many paths you can take before you need to consider bankruptcy as a remedy. When you have exhausted all of your possibilities and have made the decision to file, you can learn about the process as we outline it for you in this book. Before you move ahead into the details, take time to be proud that you are staring your monster down. You are turning on the closet light to see what is really lurking inside. Your debt is of your creation, but the monster grows stronger in your imagination and might not be as bad as it seems.

Commend yourself for having the courage to pick up this book. You have decided to do something to help yourself. You may feel that you do not have a choice, but everything is a choice. Many people sit back and wait for things to happen to them without initiating a positive first step.

Bankruptcy exists as an opportunity for you to turn your life around so you can get a fresh start. If you qualify for Chapter 7 where your debts are wiped out or Chapter 13 where some of the debts are wiped out and you make a reasonable plan for repayment, you will find that you can clean up your financial mess with dignity and closure.

So cheer up. It isn't going to be horrible. There are other people who share your problems who then go on to make changes that will prevent financial distress in the future.

## ARE YOU A CANDIDATE FOR BANKRUPTCY?

Before you can go any further, you need to consider if you are a candidate for bankruptcy filing. There are many factors to consider. Here is a list of possible signs that a bankruptcy might be right for you.

You know it is time to file for bankruptcy when:

- You pay for fast food with a credit card.
- Thieves won't even take your credit cards.
- The salesperson gives your card back to you cut into pieces.
- Your child thinks your real name is "declined."
- You don't go out before you check which credit card is "working."
- You tell creditors you are not home so many times you might as well put out a missing person's report on yourself.
- You start getting unsolicited advertisements from credit card companies that say, "don't even think about it."
- Your friends and relatives simultaneously change their phone numbers.
- You have to scrape together change from your couch seats to buy this book.

Many bankruptcies are a simple matter of filing the right forms and showing up. At the end of this book, we have included examples of forms to fill out if you are interested in filing your own case. We even walk you through the process of filling out forms in Chapter 7 by showing you what a completed form looks like and what will be expected of you. However, we do not recommend that you file bankruptcy without at least consulting an attorney. You have spent money on far more useless things in your past. This is money well spent, particularly if your case involves a house, significant assets, or issues with the IRS. Even if your case is simple, the advice you receive from a professional will help you move through the system with some doable plan for your future.

Don't drive yourself crazier than you probably already are feeling. There are nuances to the bankruptcy process and laws that may be better left to someone who understands them. You don't really want to have to know everything about bankruptcy unless it is really exciting and stimulating for you. This book gives you enough of a working knowledge of bankruptcy to ask the right questions or to be able to decide to file on your own.

Whether or not you file on your own, you have many decisions to make. There are things you can do to plan ahead for your filing. There are decisions to make regarding what filing you want to make. This book will give you the information you need to do these things. It will give you the confidence to proceed along whatever course you choose to put order back into your financial life.

Remember that no matter what the details of the bankruptcy filing, the most difficult aspect of the process is what is happening between your ears—in your head. If you can keep perspective and avoid the traps of guilt, humiliation, blame, and second-guessing, you can get through without as much damage to the life you have beyond finances. Think of it this way: Lack of money caused by a mountain of debt affects your most primal needs of security, shelter, and sustenance. Bankruptcy has definite unpleasant repercussions, but there is nothing as terrible as what you will do to yourself if you panic.

## TAKING THE FIRST STEP TOWARD FINANCIAL FREEDOM

Think of this as a new adventure. If you are hitting financial rock bottom, it certainly can't get any worse. It has to get better. It will get better. The bankruptcy laws are designed to help debtors (that means you) get back on their feet so they can restore themselves to a stable quality of life. Having to file for bankruptcy protection may feel humiliating at first, but facing and taking charge of your life is liberating.

By the way, any person facing bankruptcy gets embarrassed and feels humiliated. Some people have a personal ethic that "no one in my family files bankruptcy." What are you going to do when your creditors are hounding you and filing for judgments because you can no longer pay your bills? Put aside your pride. Get over the family tradition. In an earlier time, there wasn't as much opportunity to strangle yourself in debt. Our generation has it down to a science. Perhaps the next generation will learn from our mistakes, but rest assured, they will surely develop many problems of their own.

In this chapter, you are going to learn about the basic process of bankruptcy. The best option for you is to try to avoid bankruptcy if at all possible. Sometimes it seems as if there is no alternative when, in fact, for some people there is. When you see everything crashing in on you, you may want a quick and easy solution. Bankruptcy is one of the quicker of the legal procedures you may encounter in your life, but its effect will be felt for many years to come. The decision making and information gathering is what is most important in the preparation of your case. The actual filing and bankruptcy procedure is the most clear-cut aspect of the process.

As we said earlier, when you are in financial decline, you may believe that your circumstances are far worse than they really are. Sometimes, you may actually be in a position where a little negotiating with creditors can help you out of the mess you find yourself in. Creditors want to be paid. If you can't pay a bill, call them about it. They may give you a hard time or they may give you the option of making payments on your debt. One couple told me that they decided to stop proceeding toward bankruptcy when they found they could negotiate with their creditors, paying out small amounts on a regular basis.

On one particularly financially overwhelming day, this couple decided to stop paying their mortgage because they couldn't figure out how they could keep up with everything. They figured their credit would be shot anyway, so at least they would have some triage.

In the middle of the month, the phone rang and the person on the other end asked, "Is Mr. So and So at home?" He was standing next to his wife, but she said, "No, he isn't." The caller went on, "Is this Mrs. So and So?" She felt caught so she said, "Yes, . . ." Her usual way of handling calls like this was to say, "I am busy, or I have a kid hanging off the roof, and have to go now!" But for some reason, she hesitated, giving her caller a chance to speak.

The voice on the other line was a representative of the mortgage company. She gulped when the woman asked when they should expect the payment. She replied honestly, "I am not sure when we can pay, we are having some financial difficulty this month." She expected to be yelled at or scolded, but the woman asked, "Why are you unable to pay the bill?"

Mrs. So and So was caught off guard by this seeming statement of concern, and simply stated the truth, painful though it was, "We don't have the money this month."

What surprised her was that the person from the mortgage company then suggested a series of mechanisms for her to stay out of arrears. She was willing to offer a payment plan and even gave a month's grace period.

For this couple, the willingness of their mortgage company to offer options kept them from hiding from their creditors, waiting for their circumstances to make choices for them. They were fortunate because the extra help was enough to push them away from the necessity for declaring bankruptcy.

The mortgage company representative, though well trained in customer service, was not doing this couple a personal favor. This was a sound business decision on the mortgage company's part. The mortgage company benefits from maintaining the mortgage. The mortgage is typically front-end loaded, that is, interest payments are paid first, so that is the profit part of the mortgage. If, instead, they foreclosed, they would sell the house to realize the amount of the loan, losing all possible interest payments. It is to the advantage of the creditor to be paid by you so if you are in a position to rearrange your finances to pay your debts, your creditor may try to make it possible for you to do so. You will get cooperation from creditors if you clearly state your intention to pay and directly face your responsibilities. This assumes, of course, that you have the money to do so. No one wants to be out of money. If you are without any resources to pay even partial payments, you will have to look into other options.

## MANAGING YOUR CRISIS

There are many tactics you can use to manage your financial crises without having to go through bankruptcy. Before we look at the specifics of bankruptcy or the preliminary ways you can work with your debt, we will review the extent of the emotional upheaval you are likely to be experiencing at this time. It is important to consider this because it is going to be the worst part of the experience and your ability to navigate these waters will improve your ability to endure and move ahead.

Financial disruption is one of the most common reasons for the break down of families. It wrecks havoc on individuals. This is not a problem to be taken lightly. If you do not have awareness of what you are facing, it is going to be much worse than it has to be.

This book gives you a basic understanding of the process and implications of the remedy of bankruptcy for overwhelming debt. However, you need to look beyond the information we are giving you and the legal aspects into how this entire experience is going to affect everyone in your household.

Although individuals find it painful to go through this process, financial difficulty is most difficult for couples, especially those with children. All people come into relationships with issues around money. Some people are liberal spenders while others are more frugal. If couples have differing views of money management and there are money problems, there is a tremendous opportunity for blame and the destruction of the relationship.

### *Keep a Clear Head*

It is very important to keep a clear head and to consider the process of achieving financial health, whether it be through the filing of bankruptcy, or through some of the other opportunities available, as a shared journey. There are many important lessons to be learned through such a challenging experience and for some, although it is hard to believe, the crisis of hardship and eventual bankruptcy have been a blessing in disguise.

A downturn in finances can make you feel panicked. If you are someone who has managed to live in a reasonable and comfortable manner until an unexpected change of circumstances, you can't help but feel shock and desperation. This makes you far more vulnerable to self-defeating choices if you are feeling backed against a wall. Otherwise, honest people will find themselves lying and manipulating just to avoid the shame they feel and the disappointment of those who depend on them. Men have always held themselves to a personal standard of "provider" even if their life partner is more financially successful. A partner's success is not necessarily an issue; the larger issue is the sense of failure a man feels when he knows he can't provide for the basic needs of his family.

Many women, even if they have thriving careers, expect their spouses or mates to be the providers and will not respect a man if he fails in that role. Even if it is not a big issue to her, a slight sense of disappointment may become a monstrous accusation to a man who already is condemning himself as worthless to his family.

Mark, a man in his forties, was so afraid that his wife would be disappointed in him that he kept from her the important fact that they were getting deeper and deeper into debt. Nina, his wife, was a stay-at-home mom who had deferred financial matters to her husband. Mark was self-employed and was having trouble with his receivables. Business was down by at least half and had been for at least six months. He was taking cash advances and borrowing from Peter to pay Paul, but he didn't tell his wife a thing. He wanted her and their two children to live in the fantasy that everything was fine and there were no financial problems he could not manage. He thought he could hide the problems until business picked up again.

When Nina happened to intercept the mail one day, she found a notice of impending foreclosure on their house. She broke all speed records on the way to his office, threw it under his nose, and yelled "When were you planning to tell me about this?" Now that his secret was out in the open, he poured out all of their problems.

Nina was furious. She wasn't furious about the circumstances, as Mark had expected her to be, she was furious that he had not told her what was happening in their lives, and she was angry at herself for not asking.

This was a couple in a crisis. When Nina looked back on things, she was frustrated because she was unaware of the reality of their financial insecurity. She wished she could take back all of the frivolous spending that she had enjoyed without concern. She had blindly relied on her husband who was all too willing to take the role of family hero. They both realized that they should have been honest, open, involved, and working as a team. Not knowing, Nina had used credit or wrote checks under the assumption that there was money to pay the bills. Mark hardly paid attention to what bills were even coming in. It was a mess but not one that was uncommon. It is what we call the *blind budget system.*

This couple went through a Chapter 7 bankruptcy, which, as you will see, was the best choice for them, and had to start over. By the time they filed for bankruptcy, they had little or nothing to liquidate to pay off creditors but were able to reinstate the loan on their house and were able to rebuild their lives together. Financial upheaval was a blessing in disguise for this couple. They were forced to change their ways, pull together after the blame-and-shame stuff blew over, and reinvent how they were going to deal with money from then on.

Financial problems cause an inordinate amount of stress. When Nina considered how she and Mark had been relating to one another for at least a year before the bankruptcy, she was surprised she hadn't noticed that he had changed in his outlook on things. Her husband had become increasingly depressed, short-fused, and withdrawn, but he was too ashamed to tell her what was going on.

If they had already had their marriage "business" set up as a joint effort, they would have had better communication about exactly what was going on before it got so out of hand. Perhaps Nina could have helped by getting a part-time job. Mark had too much pride to anticipate their difficulty when they still had time to do something about it. Toward the end of the book, we are going to discuss ways to set up budgets and develop better family communication so you can rebuild a financially healthy home. No one wants to go through this experience twice if it can be helped. Once is already too much.

In the next chapter, we suggest possible ways to head bankruptcy off before it is too late. But before you look into these alternatives, it would be helpful for you to know what bankruptcy protection is and what it is not. This will educate you in your decision making. While we have provided you with relevant forms and an explanation of how they can be filled out and filed, we strongly urge you to seek legal counsel because it will likely save money in the long run. There are nuances in preparation and there is potential for claims to be disallowed that a layperson will not be able to determine.

## A FEDERAL CASE

Have you heard the expression of "don't make a federal case out of it?" Well in the case of bankruptcy, go right ahead. Bankruptcy is governed by the laws of the United States Code, which means that it is administered through the federal courts. Filing for bankruptcy relief means submitting a petition to the federal courts asking the court to consider your entire financial situation, and to either:

- Receive a legal excuse of why you no longer have to pay your debts, basically wiping out your debt as in a Chapter 7 discharge in bankruptcy or
- Force your creditors to accept a payment plan wherein they will receive only a portion of what you actually owe them. This is called a Chapter 13 bankruptcy.

There are exceptions and conditions with regard to which of your debts are dischargeable, meaning which ones can be wiped away or reduced, and which are not. These are discussed in later chapters. There are specific reasons why you would want to file under a specific chapter rather than another because there are advantages and disadvantages to each. In addition, both chapters may not be available to you.

Bankruptcies are seldom simple and straightforward, so you would be wise to ask for advice from a qualified practitioner. There are people who will charge you to fill out the forms, but they are not lawyers and cannot go to court with you. There may be complications with your case that you can't anticipate. A consultation will help you see if you fall into that category. Then you can make an informed decision if you want to accept the calculated risk of filing for bankruptcy on your own.

## ARE ALL BANKRUPTCY ATTORNEYS THE SAME?

Don't be afraid to ask to see your attorney's resume. Ask for a referral from a satisfied client. You will have to air your financial laundry with your attorney. Talk to the prospective attorney on the phone before you go in. If you don't feel good about the conversation, trust your instincts. This process is stressful enough without thinking your attorney is an idiot or, worse yet, a jerk. When people look for divorce lawyers they typically ask, "Who will go for blood?" Without considering the societal issues associated with that practice, be assured that you do not need this kind of barracuda for bankruptcy.

When you look for a bankruptcy attorney, you want someone who is knowledgeable, aware of the changes in the law, articulate, and pleasant enough not to annoy the bankruptcy trustee who has the key to your future. You also want an attorney who is not going to scare you half to death. A good bankruptcy attorney should be savvy enough to analyze what the best strategies are for you. Your attorney should help you to feel confident that at some time in the future all will be well. If you receive arrogance, judgment, or a lot of tsk tsk-ing, go to someone else.

You are the consumer. After reading this book, you should know enough to ask questions that will help you determine if your prospective attorney knows his or her business. There are many ways to find potential attorneys. The local bar association can make referrals, but be aware that many of these referrals will be of new attorneys who may not have much experience. If your case is not contested, meaning that no one is going to fight about anything, a fairly new attorney could be a good choice. A new attorney will work extra hard, give you a lot of personal attention, will be most current in the law, will charge less, and is not burnt out. He or she might be a little rough around the edges, but you can usually look beyond that.

Many people use the Yellow Pages to find a lawyer. Twenty years ago or so, lawyers were not permitted to advertise according to the Bar Code of Ethics. As this changed, it opened opportunities for otherwise disenfranchised practitioners who were not part of the "network." However, there is no real way to determine the quality of the lawyer by their advertisement. The yellow pages can be a resource but keep in mind that it is "buyer beware." Large ads that promise a lot can be enticing, but do your research before being dazzled by who can make the loudest graphic splash. Although lawyers are held to a standard of practice, there was a good reason why lawyers were not permitted to advertise.

Don't rely on an attorney's marketing ability to determine the quality of his or her work. Remember, one of the major criteria you want to use in choosing an attorney is how comfortable you feel with the person and how much he or she involves you in the decisions that will affect your life. Many attorneys have the attitude, "I know how to do this and you don't, so let me do it and don't bother me about it." That is not the attitude that you want your attorney to have.

*Don't Be a Nuisance*

You do not want to make yourself a nuisance by calling several times a day with millions of questions and concerns. If you feel the need to be neurotic, call a friend. If you are taking too much advantage of your lawyer's time, you may actually be preventing him or her from working on your behalf. However, you should feel comfortable with your meetings. You should leave each meeting with your attorney with a sense of empowerment that you know what is going on. You don't have to know every detail. But you should know what decisions you are actually making, what the implications will be for your life, and what alternatives you might have. If you want to come out of this experience with a better chance of moving your life ahead, you would be wise to participate in the process as much as possible.

As you can see, we are pretty insistent in suggesting that anyone considering filing bankruptcy should at least consult an attorney even if one is not retained. Bankruptcy involves a court proceeding. Although it is simple if the case is simple, it will be less intimidating if you have someone with you who understands the procedure.

Most lawyers can handle bankruptcy cases that are simple and direct. If you know your case will be complicated, you may want to seek a certified bankruptcy expert. You can check with your state bar association or the Internet for a list of these practitioners. These practitioners have had additional concentrated education in bankruptcy.

Here are some other reasons why it is advisable to have an attorney:

- Contrary to what many people believe about filing for bankruptcy, you do not have to lose everything you own. The courts allow for you to maintain what you need to live through specified *exemptions*. An attorney can help you maximize your outcome while walking you through the process.

- If a creditor knows you are not represented by an attorney, he might try to convince you to enter into a reaffirmation agreement, which is an agreement to repay a debt either during your bankruptcy proceeding or afterward when, due to your discharge in bankruptcy, you no longer have a legal obligation to pay. If you don't know that significant fact, you will be out of luck.

A discharge means that you do not have to pay that debt. But if you are harassed by a creditor, you can be manipulated into paying money you don't have to pay. If you are persuaded into making an agreement with a creditor after a bankruptcy discharge, this is considered a binding agreement that you will have to pay. You may be convinced that this is an honorable thing to do, but if you were in a position to pay the bill in the first place, you would not have had to file for bankruptcy.

Although we give you a comprehensive understanding of how the process works in this book, you might not know that there are situations where you might want to reinstate a debt, particularly if you want to keep the item to which the debt is associated such as a house or a car.

If you have little or no assets and you feel confident in using the forms at the end of this book, you may want to file your own bankruptcy case. Here are some ways to determine if your particular case involves issues that may be more complicated than average:

- You have taken recent cash advances or purchased luxury items.
- You have obligations owed to the Internal Revenue Service.
- You hope to discharge student loans.
- You have child support or alimony obligations.
- You have a home in foreclosure.
- You have many assets or own your own business.

If your situation is not listed above but you do not feel that you fully understand the concepts introduced in this book (such as what exemptions apply to you), then get help.

## GET GOOD HELP

You will be living with your decisions for a long time. In Chapter 4, we discuss the various options among which you, as the debtor, have to choose. Which bankruptcy chapter is appropriate for you will be based on an analysis of your financial situation: How much and who you owe, what assets you have and want to keep, what your basic expenses are, and how much income you have.

If you can, you will want to choose Chapter 7 for a complete discharge of all your debts in bankruptcy. If you have assets you want to keep and/or a mortgage in arrears or in foreclosure, nagging IRS problems that just won't go away, or other secured arrearages, you might need to seek a Chapter 13 repayment plan to keep the secured assets.

Businesses have available to them protection under Chapter 11, which is a way for them to negotiate with creditors while still operating their business. The goal is reorganization instead of closing the business. Chapter 11 does not apply to personal bankruptcy.

While you can rest assured that one way or another you will find a solution to your debt problem, you need to fight the sense of stigma that you probably feel. For everyone brave enough to get their finances under control, there are 10 people who should do something to change their circumstances. If you are in over your head, you can't have a quality of life that allows for things other than the money gerbil wheel. If you must live in a "need" mentality, you can't prosper. This will affect your relationships and every thing you do.

People may treat you a little differently if they know that you have filed for bankruptcy. This is usually a reflection of their own fear that somehow your financial statement is contagious. All of the creditors, credit card companies, and stores that used to wow you with their special offers and flattery now will want nothing to do with you. This, however, is not all bad.

Get over it. You have more important things to worry about. You never really want to know what goes on behind other people's closed doors. You definitely don't want the burden of another person's checkbook, because it may contain more devils than your own. You can spend your time and energy trying to maintain appearances or, as we have already suggested, you can dive right into the problem and put your energy into finding solutions.

## FILING EARLIER INSTEAD OF LATER IS USUALLY WISER

Some people are so filled with shame that they wait almost too long before seeking help and filing for bankruptcy. There are definite advantages to filing early that are missed if you let your fear and pride stand in the way.

If you delay filing, struggling to pay the minimum on your credit cards and in the process falling behind in your mortgage payments, you may find yourself forced to file a Chapter 13 to save your home, rather than a simple Chapter 7. Once you have reached the point where you can't afford to pay all of your basic bills and your credit cards, too, it is throwing good money after bad to continue to borrow to pay by taking consolidation loans, cash advances, and transferring your balance from one company to another to take advantage of temporary low rates for transferred balances. There are times when loans are a good way to avoid filing, but we discuss those factors in the next chapter.

You want to be in charge of your own decisions rather than allowing circumstances to make them for you.

As you will see, a Chapter 13 bankruptcy can be the best situation for you if, for example, you owe the Internal Revenue Service a lot of money from past business or tax returns. Chapter 13 could actually be the miracle you are looking for. Under a Chapter 13, if you have IRS obligations more than three years old you may only have to pay them off to the extent of the assets that you own. There are many ways to get on your feet even when circumstances look most grim.

Another big advantage to filing early is that filing for bankruptcy creates what is called *an automatic stay*. What this means is that all of your debts are essentially frozen during the pendency of your case. Although there are some debts such as utilities that are not affected by the automatic stay, there are many advantages to not having to pay credit cards and other loan payments while you are in the process of reassessing your entire financial future. You may have some of these debts discharged, so the automatic stay gives you some breathing room and time where you do not have to pay toward something that may eventually be forgiven. If you are filing for bankruptcy, it is obvious you are in difficult financial circumstances. Don't think the court never gives you a break.

Filing bankruptcy will stop the creditors from calling you and trying to intimidate you into paying your bills. While your case is pending, your automatic stay stops your creditors from being able to collect from you, with certain exceptions and conditions. For example, if you have money deposited in a financial institution where you also have an unpaid balance on a loan, the institution is permitted to take the balance on deposit and apply it to your debt. This rule applies whether or not you file for bankruptcy, so be advised that if you are going to default on a loan where you have a deposit account, you should remove those funds prior to default or bankruptcy.

If you have overdue utility bills, the automatic stay prevents the utility company from cutting off your services for 20 days after filing. However, at the end of the grace period, the utility company can require you to pay a deposit or cut off your services for nonpayment.

You are still obligated on such things as your mortgage (assuming you intend to keep your house). Except for your mortgage and utilities, you can plug your phone back in and stop wearing the disguise you have been hiding behind to avoid the possibility that a creditor will recognize you. You may as well go out of your house on occasion. There is no scarlet "D" on your clothing accusing and condemning you as a "deadbeat."

Being able to look at options and having an automatic stay on your bills so you can assess your situation are two advantages of facing your financial crisis honestly and calmly. As you well know, if you are not careful, money troubles can become your identity. Think about how much energy we expend and the lengths we go to maintain our financial house of cards when we see it about to fall. We juggle creditors by charging on one card to pay the minimum on another. We train our children to say, "He is not home." One woman made a game of it. When a creditor called, she answered the phone, "I am not home," and hung up. *This is not how you want to live.*

If we have been maintaining a certain lifestyle and experience financial turmoil, we try to avoid social situations, but it isn't always possible. We feel obligated to keep up appearances. We know one man who continued to go out with his financially secure friends and tried to keep up with their lifestyle, one he had enjoyed for many years. He had been living beyond his means for a long time, but now he wasn't able to keep a wad of cash in his wallet. Before leaving his house, he would check his available credit but if he reached for the check, as he was apt to do, he would sweat until the waitperson returned with the credit slip for his signature, worrying that it would be declined.

What he didn't realize was that his friends would not have wanted him to go through this torment. He was being unfair to them as well as himself.

In our current economy, everyone is feeling the crunch. If you are not independently wealthy, and sometimes even if you are, times are tough. We all have been living too well for the past decade or so without feeling the backlash of our financial choices. The impact of 9/11 will influence our economy for many years to come. In this decade, for many people, credit is being maxed, our savings are diminished or nonexistent, and our stocks are nothing anyone wants to discuss in public. The financial frolic we have enjoyed needs to be reigned in and we have to mature. It is no fun, but it was bound to happen sooner or later.

## CHANGE IS INEVITABLE

Just as many of us are ready to throw in the towel and accept our medicine, the legislature is trying to reform the entire process. Although we do not know exactly if and when the reform will pass, some practitioners say it is simply a matter of time. For the purposes of this book, we try to explain how the reforms may influence a certain aspect of your process. This book is comprehensive but cannot substitute for more advanced treatment of the subject. We focus on the basics of bankruptcy. As we said earlier, however, you might want to pay particular attention to ways you can avoid bankruptcy in case you find yourself in a situation where you do not qualify at all. The reform will make it more difficult to file certain cases. Be prepared.

Even with the anticipated changes, the basics of bankruptcy will remain much the same. In the last chapter of the book, we explain how the reform, should it pass, will change the face of bankruptcy. You should know and note that it will be harder to file a Chapter 7 and work out a Chapter 13 plan.

Because bankruptcy is not to be taken lightly in any event, and because of the pending changes in the law, we have included a chapter on how credit works and how you might be able to dig your way out without seeking bankruptcy protection. Part of the reform will be to require debtors to have undergone credit counseling prior to filing for bankruptcy relief. This is a good idea whether or not it is legislated.

## BANKRUPTCY LAW IS INTENDED TO HELP YOU

Bankruptcy law is intended to help you, not humiliate you. It is intended to help you get a fresh start with the hope that you will learn how not to get into the same situation again. However, the process is being reformed in a way that will make it more difficult for people who are in need to get the same kind of relief that has been available in previous years. Credit card companies have a strong voice in our political environment.

While there are many reasons to believe the credit card companies are somewhat to blame for why we are finding ourselves in these predicaments, there is also support from bankruptcy trustees and judges who have frowned on those who they perceive to be playing the system. As in everything, there will always be those who deliberately attempt to manipulate the system to get a free ride in the bankruptcy courts. The reform will make bankruptcy less available for everyone who wants it and the trustees and judges will look more closely at your filing for red flags in your paperwork that arouse suspicion that there could be deliberate or careless fraud. In spite of what well-meaning friends may tell you, if you run up a lot of credit card debt, but never make any payments, or make just a few payments, your trustee and your creditor may seek to dismiss your case for fraud, because it will seem to them that you incurred debts with the knowledge that you would probably never pay them. Get rid of the attitude "What the heck, I'm going to file bankruptcy." Watch your spending. Even without reform, the trustee does not need to accept every debt for discharge.

So where are you now? You have debt with the inability to pay it. This is not cosmic. Either you made bad decisions, were stuck by unexpected circumstances, were too depressed or inebriated to watch what was happening to your finances, or a myriad of other reasons that could have gotten you to where you are. You may be like millions of other Americans, clueless as to the implications of the use of credit and how it eventually takes on a life of its own.

No matter how you got here, a problem is something that has a solution. It is only a problem and it can be solved. We even show you how you can avoid having the problem return to pull you back into its lair.

## BEYOND DEBT RELIEF

Perhaps the more important issues to consider are beyond those regarding debt relief. Financial crisis destroys families, marriages, and your spirit. Human beings are prone to drama. We are also prone to blame when we feel threatened. The actual process of bankruptcy is a lot simpler than the emotional issues and psychological upheaval that it engenders. Blame is poison to a relationship and it is inevitable in situations like this. In most situations, a couple knows that things are changing. It is difficult not to know that things are tight or that credit cards are becoming overused. However, it is not uncommon for one or another to hide or downplay spending habits. It is not uncommon for a couple to just stop talking about it as if the problem will go away on its own.

Face your financial demons head on. Bring them out into the light so they stop being those monsters under your bed and in your closet.

Nothing is worth losing your health and sanity. We all avoid the truth. We all hate the discomfort of seeing "how bad things really are." The fact is, however, that things are always worse if they are left unknown.

The life of a person or a family facing impending bankruptcy is stressful. You need to involve all family members, including children, in the process without over-burdening them. Teaching frugality is a good thing. Creating fear of money and loss in a young person or child is unfortunate. One of the worst things you can do is to try to keep up appearances for the sake of your child. Children are highly perceptive. They will pick up on your stress. It is better to say "we can't afford that now," than to be dishonest, or buy whatever it is with money you need for something else. Children will always prefer honesty and sanity to a new Nintendo, even if they nag you otherwise.

## YOU WILL SURVIVE!

You will be able to do this and you will survive. You will be amazed at how wonderful it feels to take charge of your financial life. You already know what it feels like to have no control. If you were in control, you would not be reading this book. If you did not have acute anxiety, you would not be looking at ways to salvage your future. The worst is now. Everything from now on is the road to recovery.

Bankruptcy can be a blessing. Like attending a confessional, you are able to admit past wrongs so you can receive absolution.

If you can separate the personal sense of defeat, loss, and failure from the objective fact that you have extended your liabilities far beyond your ability to pay, you can look objectively at how you can deal with the present circumstances while preparing for a brighter tomorrow.

Unless you are a masochist or self-destructive sociopath, we sincerely doubt that when you set out to buy that DVD player that you intended to take it out of your flesh with humiliation. We all need to change our attitude about spending and to learn to handle money in a way that is saner. You wouldn't be reading a book on how to file bankruptcy if you were unaware that you were in trouble. Oddly enough, sometimes bankruptcy is better than bad credit. When you are discharged in bankruptcy, your debt is wiped away. You also may not refile for seven years. Therefore, a creditor will consider you a good risk and will, after a while, extend credit to you. Not that we recommend going from the proverbial frying pan into the fire: Credit is poison to some of us. However, there are times when it is necessary. In time, you will be able to rebuild your credit worthiness. If you begin buying some small items on credit and pay everything on time, you will be stable in no time.

As we said earlier in this chapter, we commend you. If you need to file bankruptcy according to the advice and recommendations you find in this book, or even if you are able to find a way to avoid it, you are going to be better off. You will be free of spending and accumulating debt. There is freedom in knowing what you have and accepting who you are. There is freedom in the honesty it takes to face your demons and overcome them. Your willingness to face your financial picture head-on makes you the ultimate demon slayer.

# 2 | Quicksand Credit and Callous Creditors

Credit is not money. Credit means that someone or some institution loans you money, even if it is on paper, under the agreement that you will pay it back with interest. Credit cards used to be a sign of status. There is an episode of "I love Lucy" where Lucy's nemesis, a snobby old friend, shows her a wallet full of credit cards. This was meant to rub Lucy's face in the fact that the friend was better treated and supported by her husband because she could shop anywhere she wanted to.

Credit is still a sign of status of sorts, because it gives you buying power. You can have the things you want without having to earn the money ahead of time to pay for it. The problem is credit is too easy to get, and it is too easy to forget about the fact that you have to pay it back with interest. Credit cards make purchases far too enticing. Advertising tells us that if you have a gold or silver card, you are somehow more important to the world and are more successful. When you whip out that gold card to pay for dinner, you might as well be Zorro.

The problem is that credit is quicksand. If you spend ahead on it, you will surely discover that the interest you have agreed to pay makes it impossible for you to keep up. If you are not paying your balance off each month, it will not be long before you are struggling to get out of a hole that you didn't even realize was there.

## CHALLENGES FOR THE SELF-EMPLOYED

People who are self-employed are especially vulnerable to quicksand credit. If you do not know exactly how much money you are going to have at the beginning of the month, it is difficult to plan. If you have enough money so that it exceeds your overhead, you won't have a problem. But if you are living from paycheck to paycheck and you don't know how much that paycheck is going to be, you are always going to be in an endless spiral of ups and downs.

The other problem for the self-employed is that if you are living from unknown paycheck to paycheck, you are going to have to rely on credit to get you through the lean times. When you do receive a chunk of money, it is very easy to mismanage it and to channel it into things that do not necessarily include paying off your credit card balances—out-of-sight, out-of-mind. You will tend to look at your credit card balances as monthly bills without paying attention to the fact that you are not paying for the underlying debt, you are paying the interest. You are essentially paying the loan holder—the credit card company—a salary to hold onto the bill you owe them. If you think about it, who needs a creditor on the payroll.

People who are self-employed have to be very good planners. When you have a big check in hand, you can feel as if you are rich. It is easy to forget how long that check has to last. This generation, with the possible exception of those who remember the Great Depression, is "now" oriented. Self-employed people are especially vulnerable because of all of the lean times spent waiting for money and work to come in.

Self-employed people who live close to the edge of their income are very likely to use credit cards to make it from one month to the next. If you are running out of money waiting for your next big check or have receivables outstanding from your customers, you have to find a way to live. Aside from the basics of life, it is natural to want to go a little crazy when you have been living in a state of imposed frugality. But if you fire your credit company employee, you can give yourself a raise. You can plan ahead and save for the times when you want to splurge. Isn't hindsight great?

If you are self-employed and have been following the "spend-ahead-pay-later plan," don't feel bad. You are in the majority. It is very typical for people with small businesses and inconsistent earnings to live with the "I'll-worry-about-it-later," accounting system even if they continuously get themselves into trouble. The self-employed life is uncertain at best. There are ways to make it more stable as we will see in the chapter on small business structures, but it is difficult to resist the pattern of spending money before you actually have it in the bank.

## WAGE EARNER WOES

A steady income can lull a person into a false sense of security, hence, the wage earner also can have problems. One thing that has become abundantly clear in today's job climate: Even if you are in a professional or upper management position with a thriving company, nothing can ever be completely certain. We are all feeling the pinch of a changing economy. There are layoffs announced every day in the news media. In previous decades, we worked ourselves into an acquiring mentality. Now, we may have the credit to buy anything we want when we want it, but we do not necessarily have the steady income to back up this pattern of purchasing. We have access to far more credit than our income should ever allow.

Wage earners need to be realistic about what they have left to spend after taxes, social security, insurance, or whatever is taken out of the paycheck at the end of each month. Few people ever have exactly enough. The lifestyle that we are encouraged to live through the constant media barrage of consumerism couldn't possibly fit into the means of most of us.

It is a little frightening to think about who is frequenting all of the stores that are springing up like chicken pox all over America to say nothing of the myriad Internet sites that beckon to us every time we turn on the computer. There are so many things to buy that it is overwhelming. Shopping and the need for constant acquisition is like an addiction. This may be an addiction that you find yourself fighting. If you are reading this book, it is very likely that you have been sucked into the great American hobby . . . spend, spend, and spend.

There are so many ways to fall on hard times. Many people are seeking bankruptcy protection for reasons that have nothing to do with spending. Not that there is anything wrong with spending as such. We are not making a moral judgment. However, it is my opinion that overspending is the tool of the devil and credit cards are contracts on your soul. When you regain or take control of your finances, you will realize you have been living in a trance of consumerism.

## FACE THE MUSIC

You are responsible for your own choices so don't even think of saying, "the devil made me do it." Now is the time to face the music, but you will never survive the process and return to sanity if you do not accept that you are vulnerable to temptation and have to rethink how you live your life. Do you really need that super deluxe gas grill when your present grill will do the job? If you really like the new gas grill and know that you will use it and it will add quality to your life and you do not owe money to everyone else in town then by all means buy it. But bigger or newer is not necessarily better when you do not have the cash in the bank to support a purchase.

The idea is to look at the bigger picture of your finances before you give into the "I wants." Credit is so available that many of us treat it like a second job. This second job allows us to buy the things we want or to do the things we want. We will do them or have them now and then we don't have to think about it until the bills come. The minimum charges seem so low, at least, until you look at your interest charges.

We are conditioned to this attitude as if it were in our DNA. When my daughter was young, she once asked me to buy her something at a particular store and, being the overly indulgent parent that I am, I decided to avoid the situation not by saying "no" but by telling her I didn't have any money with me. She looked up at me quite innocently and said, "Well, why don't you just use a credit card?"

It is ironic that many of us will buy something we think is a wonderful bargain, something off the clearance racks, and pay for it with a credit card. Unless we pay for it immediately at the end of the month, we have just paid much more for the item than if we had bought it at the full retail price the first time around. There are no bargains if we are using credit because we are always paying for the privilege of borrowing the money ahead of time so we can do what we want right now.

Don't feel stupid about falling for the quicksand trap of credit. If you look around, it is more than obvious that you have plenty of company. Many people today are experiencing the same anxiety and financial woes as you. Our country has been in crisis since before 9/11, the stock market has taken a nosedive, and more people than you would think have tapped out their credit lines. We have our vision of the good life and it is difficult to change it.

What is different now is that many people who have used credit as an extension of their lifestyle have had secure jobs that have provided the income level to support the cards. We all can blame ourselves if we have been less than responsible about our spending. But now with the changes in the economy, people have been hit with all types of unexpected changes.

Many people at high levels of the corporate ladder are losing their jobs. Not all of them are getting a golden parachute, contrary to what the media tell us. When you have worked hard all of your life and have paid your dues climbing the corporate ladder only to be hit in the face with a layoff or downsizing demotion, it can be devastating. We all have our expectations of the good life. When you have been able to maintain a high standard of living without the use of smoke and mirrors, it can be even more shocking to have the rug pulled out from under you.

This is why the limited use of credit is advisable even for those who have worked their way into the sphere of the "haves." Anything can happen and will happen at any time. Too much extended credit is a prison sentence for anyone. You do not need multiple credit cards. Get rid of them, hide them, or cancel them. Somehow, reduce the sheer number of cards you have available to you.

## HOOKING THE YOUNG CONSUMER

Credit is too abundant. Everyone including my dog (some people have had cards sent to their pets—honest!) receives preapproved credit cards. The biggest travesty is how easy it is for college students to receive credit cards long before they even know how to do their own laundry. We may need to change our ways in how we teach our children about laundry and handling money, but students are vulnerable when they have their first taste of freedom. We are not with them 24 hours each day so we are going to have to prepare them for the barrage of credit opportunities that will be at their door. They have to be prepared to say, "No, thanks!" and mean it.

Credit card companies make it easy for young people to obtain credit and they tempt them with special offers. Children learn to spend against future wealth even before they figure out what they want to be when they grow up. This is ironic when you realize that the bankruptcy reform is supported mainly by credit card companies so they will not be in such a position of loss when someone files for relief. Perhaps parents need to lobby for reform so that credit card companies are forced to stop freely marketing to those people, often children, who do not even have an income.

There is a tremendous rise in bankruptcy filings for young people under the age of 24. These young people are lured in without the tools to understand how credit works in reality, in the fine print, and as a result, they will be saddled with the inability to obtain legitimate credit worthiness when they are mature enough to handle it.

Even with the very high incidence of bankruptcies filed each year, including an ever-rising percentage of bankruptcies filed by people in their early twenties, the income of credit card companies far exceeds their losses. Credit cards are essentially high interest loans extended to you by banks, stores, and gasoline stations. Remember that these cards are designed to make you feel that if you have a large credit line, that you have an excess of money.

## WHEN INTEREST ACCUMULATES FASTER THAN INCOME

When you buy everything with a credit card, it is almost impossible to pay the minimum every month. If you pay your complete balance each month, you are okay because you don't have to worry about penalties or interest. But few people are able to do this. If you are using your card to buy something because you forgot the cash or are waiting for a check, it seems likely that you can and will pay your full amount when the bill comes due.

If you are looking at credit as a way to have today what you can't actually afford, it is very unlikely that you will be able to pay off your balance as it becomes due. The average American lives paycheck to paycheck without much focus on saving.

We typically don't do what our parents or grandparents did. We do not save up for the things we want. We also don't hold on to things. In our parents' time, it would have been unheard of to buy new furniture every few years to satisfy a decorating whim. You bought good furniture when you could afford it and it would stay with you for the rest of your life or at least as long as it remained useable.

People who buy things on credit are actually the darlings of the economy. Banks love us. They thrive on us. Banks don't like those people who buy things and pay off their credit card balance at the end of each month. Banks do not value people who only use their credit cards for purchases off the Internet or from infomercials and who pay them off right away. People who are in control of their spending probably do not spend too much time buying on the Internet anyway. Forget infomercials. Some people are born with spending discipline. Unfortunately, my children have inherited the shopping DNA. My daughter is always running up to me with the news, "if you buy it in the next five minutes they will send you two!"

Keep in mind how credit cards actually work. The interest on credit cards alone accounts for 75 percent of the profits earned by banks that issue credit cards (*Money Troubles, Legal Strategies to Cope with Your Debts*, Robin Leonard, Nolo Press, 1997).

If you look carefully at your credit card agreements after the introductory rate when the interest amount applies, you will see that if you max it out, it will probably take you until your great grandchildren are born to pay it off. This is, of course, if you are paying the minimum amounts required each month. If you look further, you will see that the amount you owe will continue to expand exponentially the longer you maintain the loan. It is like swimming upstream. Eventually you run out of energy and drown, which is what has brought you to this book.

## IN OVER YOUR HEAD

The U.S. bankruptcy laws were established on the principle that people who inadvertently get in over their heads can find a way to dig themselves out. As we have already discussed, the biggest reason people file bankruptcy is because they are overwhelmed with credit card debt. It is important to note that with the reform, it will be much more difficult to discharge much of this debt. This is why you will want to consider how you can get out from under some of your debt before you have no other choice but to file.

The good news is that you have many options that can help you reduce your debt before filing, which will help your ultimate result. Although bankruptcy is a reasonable option in that it affords a way out from under the load of debt, make sure you understand credit and your obligations so you can rid yourself of as much debt as you reasonably can. You will also want to rebuild your credit, cautiously after all this trouble, and you will want to avoid this mess in the future.

The first thing you need to do is to stop, cease, and desist from spending on credit. Put those cards in a drawer under lock and key. Cut them up if you can. Save one or two with small balances and pay them off. Do not max out your cards if you can avoid it. The more credit you have maxed, the more difficult some of these remedies can be. You owe the money. The more you add, the more you owe. If you are not discharged in bankruptcy, you still owe it. It may be possible to pay and avoid the exorbitant interest rates, but don't assume that you can get out from under the debt altogether. After all, you do have all of the items you have purchased and have already eaten all of the food you charged. You don't plan on returning it, do you?

If you stop spending on credit, you can begin to pay off your credit cards in a reasonable manner. Learn to use cash for your purchases. If you file bankruptcy, you are going to have to do everything on a cash basis anyway. If you are able to work out reasonable payments that will get you out from under your credit card debt, you will change your ways, and get a fresh start but you will still preserve your credit. Having a good credit rating can be a good thing. You will want to have it again. Right now having a lot of credit and a lot of debt serves no one, especially you. So, get rid of as much as you can.

If you are performing bill-paying triage, you may not have a clear picture of what you owe. If you are paying the minimum of one credit card at the middle of the month, the minimum of another at the beginning of the month or whenever you have the money, you may find that you are further behind than you think. You are going to have to look specifically at the big picture to design a way out.

## SURMOUNTING THE DEBT MOUNTAIN

The most basic consideration is whether or not your expenses far exceed your ability to pay. I know one couple who spent less and less until they felt that they were spending virtually nothing. Their income should have been enough for an average family of four to live modestly. They pulled together all of their bills to look at the global picture and were astounded. When they put all of their expenses and liabilities together on a big chart, they saw clearly that they couldn't possibly keep up with their mountain of debt.

More likely than not, when you place all of the credit card minimums end to end you will be amazed by how many times they will wrap around your neck. Get a clear picture of your total expenses and liabilities. When you can't meet the minimum payments on your credit cards, it is time to do something about it. There is still hope where there is still some income beyond the basics, such as housing, utilities, and food.

One game people play is to take the low interest offers of a new card and transfer all of their debt from another card to it to reduce the monthly bill. This wastes a lot of energy and time because you are still going to wind up back where you started. It is best to look at the larger picture and to create a strategy of how to dig your way out.

One of the first things you can try to do is to refinance your home. If you are able to do this, you can actually have the cash to pay off your credit cards in one lump sum so that you incorporate the payments into a single payment each month. You will essentially be using the equity in your home to pay off your mortgage and will then be creating a new loan that includes the amount you need to pay off your bills. It is a lot simpler than it sounds.

The advantage to this is that any credit card or consumer debt is going to invariably be at a higher interest rate than a mortgage. If you have equity in your home, you could potentially refinance the mortgage to a higher amount and take the difference in cash. You can pay your debts and extend the length of or the monthly payment of your mortgage. Another advantage to this is that your mortgage payments are tax deductible. Your credit card payments are not. If you are buried under consumer debt and are able to pay only the minimums, this may be a good option.

Be aware, however, that you do not automatically qualify for refinancing simply because you have equity in your home. The bank will also consider what kind of risk you are. If you are having financial difficulties already to the extent that you are late with all of your payments, you may very likely be turned down or will not be given a rate that would help you anyway.

Just because you are in over your head does not mean you should pay things late. You should try to intervene before you absolutely can't pay your debts so you will have more options available to you. Watch if you are having trouble making your minimum payments. Early intervention as is suggested for many terminal illnesses can give you a much more optimistic prognosis for your debt illness as well.

The time to consider refinancing your home is before you are really buried under consumer debt. If you see that things are getting tight and you are feeling pressured, look into it right away. There is a point of no return after which debt explodes. After that, there is no stopping it from consuming everything in its way including you.

A second option for you if you see ahead of time that your consumer debt monster is growing bigger than you can handle is a home equity line of credit. This is where you borrow against your home equity in the form of a second mortgage. You can use the money any way you like, but the wise thing to do would be to pay your debts or as many as you can with this money so you only have one payment to make each month instead of nine. Yes, many people pay on nine credit cards per month or even more. You know who you are. You can also pay off other debts to clear them from your overhead.

The advantage to this much like the refinance option is that your second mortgage will be payable at a much lower interest rate than your credit cards or store financing accounts. It will be an entirely separate payment from your first mortgage, but it will still be ultimately more efficient.

The downside of using the equity in your home to obtain a second mortgage to pay off credit card debt is that most people who do this inevitably forget that this new amount they are paying represents the mountain of credit card debt that they had built up, and turn right around and run up a new mountain of debt. Then they are stuck with both the larger mortgage(s) and the new credit card debt. The result? Even if they qualify to discharge the credit card debt in bankruptcy, they are stuck with the bloated mortgage if they wish to keep their home.

With a home equity loan, you are able to take up to 100 percent of the equity in your home. If you do consolidate your debt either through refinancing or through a second mortgage, you will have a big advantage if you want to preserve your credit because you will only have one bill. You will be able to pay it on time, which is an important factor in determining your creditworthiness.

If you are already in the throes of the debt vortex, you may not qualify for either of these means of debt consolidation. You will be evaluated as a viable risk for a home equity line of credit or anything of this nature. The loan officer and the underwriters are going to look at your credit score. This is a figure that is determined by looking at your overall financial picture to determine your creditworthiness based on factors that fit within a formula.

## DECIPHERING THE BEACON SCORE

Every time you are considered for credit, a potential creditor is going to look at what is called your *beacon score*. This is a number score that is based on many factors that provide a relatively consistent method for creditors to determine how risky it will be to loan you money and evaluates their chances of collecting on that loan once it is made. They are all happy to give you credit when you are starting out, but if you want credit after you have been given enough time to mess it up, forget it.

Having a credit score in itself seems like a good reason to feel inadequate. Credit scoring can make you feel as if there are these mysterious know-it-all people gossiping behind your back judging your worth as a person. They are probably the grown-up versions of bullies in school. Of course, they save these people to work for the IRS. (Just kidding, IRS. We have great respect for your power over us.)

Don't let this credit scoring stuff upset you. It is a number, nothing more, and it is a fact of life. If you want someone to loan you money, they have a right to know who you are. If you want to avoid this, you should consider the advantages of stuffing your money in your mattress.

The beacon score is a number ranging from 400 up to 850. Don't assume a person with a Lexus has a high score. The score is made up of many factors. The score takes into account how well you repay loans or pay your credit cards, how many types of credit items you have, such as furniture loans, car loans, or credit cards, length of time you have had a card or a loan, whether or not you pay your bills on time, and how many times you have had someone access your credit. A good part of the score will take into account information gathered by the three major credit reporting agencies that you will learn more about in a later chapter. These reports show everything. This is why bill collectors like to threaten that an unpaid bill will be reflected on your credit report. It will.

When the beacon score takes into consideration the data as reflected in your credit report, it weighs everything related to your credit history. It does not just include the negative stuff. So, if you do something good like pay off at least some of your cards monthly, this will contribute favorably to your score. Remember, beacon scores especially like payments that are made on time and if you have less debt. That is why consolidation is good if you can get it.

You may not realize it but each time you apply for a credit card, the credit card company pulls a credit report. The fact that they even checked your credit becomes points taken off your overall score. So if you are playing the "let's see how much credit we can have in one lifetime game," you are causing trouble for yourself in the long run that you might not even know about. Even if you do not ever use that credit, the fact that you have it can be a negative and the fact that you asked for it can be a negative.

If you want to have credit or want to be able to buy a house, you will be very happy if you have an overall beacon score of 700 or better. If you have a score of 600 or less it might not be easy to get a loan or you might only qualify for one with a high interest rate. Buying a home or applying for a sizeable loan such as one to support or start a business is where you are going to feel the repercussions of a low beacon score the most. As we said, scores typically range from 400 to 850. The average is typically somewhere around 720. If you want to get a mortgage or loan from a top bank, you will probably need a score of at least 640. The closer you are to those higher numbers, the better the interest rate. But don't despair, you can seek a loan from a bank that is not first rate with a higher interest if you have a score of 540 or above.

Don't spend too much time dwelling on the all powerful beacon score. It is a fact of life. But it is not the only factor.

## YOU HAVE SOME OTHER OPTIONS

If you are on the verge of bankruptcy, you may be most concerned with holding on to what you have without being too concerned with the nuances of your credit future. There is another option for you before you choose to file for bankruptcy. There are many highly qualified and helpful credit-counseling services that can help you get on your feet.

Although credit-counseling services can't help everyone, they can help many people in your situation. The best thing about credit-counseling services, depending on the individual you work with, is they do not tend to make you feel stupid. Their goal is to help you get out from under your financial troubles and to educate you about how to manage your money in the future. The beauty of credit-counseling services is that they understand what much of our society does not, that money management is not an instinct like procreation. It is something that can and should be taught especially as our monetary systems become more complex.

If you are already showing an inability to pay your debts, you can be proactive in helping your situation by finding a nonprofit service such as through the Internet Web site: www.moneymanagement.org. We recommend using a nonprofit organization for many reasons, not the least of which is if someone offers to do this for you for a fee, you would be better off using that money to pay some of your outstanding debts. Nonprofits are funded through grants, donations, or sponsorships. They may even be supported by for-profit credit-counseling organizations, but their work is to provide you with a service and an education. There are for-profit counseling services that are legitimate. Just be careful that you do not fall for big promises of lots of money. Sometimes a sense of desperation makes us throw logic out the window.

Credit counseling is not for everyone, but if you are not too far into debt, you will do well with some help. As an example, the mission statement of one money management counseling agency as it is stated on their Web site is that they are "professional, certified counselors [who] will evaluate your financial state, assist in creating a spending plan, and negotiate the terms of your debts with creditors. By negotiating terms such as lower interest rates and waived late fees, they can often provide you with more affordable payments and a shorter payoff period. We will consolidate all of your unsecured debts into one convenient monthly deposit that will disburse directly to your creditors." You pay a certain amount to them each month that is put into a FDIC insured trust account to be used to pay your creditors directly.

There are many credit-counseling services to choose from. There are advertisements on television appealing to people in financial distress. You need to find out up front if the service is nonprofit and you need to determine the qualifications of the people you will be working with. You want to know if the agency is accredited to do what they do. You should be able to ask for their references or their organization information and should be given everything you ask for without any hesitation. What you are trying to determine is if they are reputable. You want to make sure that the information you give them is confidential. If the service is reputable, there is no question that they have a duty to you to keep your records and the content of your meetings private.

A counseling service should be helpful in terms of determining what you could actually afford to pay each month. When they derive a formula, they will negotiate with your creditors on your behalf to see if they can have some of the penalties reduced on your accounts. They may even be able to help you settle on particular amounts with your creditors. Remember that your creditors want to be paid. That is the bottom line for them. They want to be paid as much of the debt as possible and would prefer this to having you go belly up.

One of the best advantages of a credit counseling service of this kind is that you write one check or money order to them each month and they take care of divvying it up among your creditors. This is worth everything in the world to someone who is hanging on to their financial sanity by their teeth.

These services have helped many people get back on their feet. The best use of them would be to seek help before the mountain of debt piles up. Many of them provide credit and budget education so you can learn to manage finances before you are into crisis management.

When you work with credit counseling, the next issue for you may be whether or not you can continue to pay the payment as derived with the credit counselor without eliminating your ability to live with any quality of life. If you are sacrificing too much and are still struggling painfully, you will want to consider bankruptcy. There comes a point where you just have to give in and make a rational decision by weighing the pros and cons. Do it on paper. Look your complete financial situation square in the eye and make your best possible decision.

## AVOIDING JUDGMENTS

Another touchstone consideration is whether you are in immediate danger of having your assets attached, liened, or garnished because of a bad debt. When you can't pay your debts, your creditors can go to court and get judgments against you. Some of them can actually take a legal interest in certain types of property you have. Some creditors can "garnish your wages" where they legally cause your employer to pay a certain amount to them each month directly out of your paycheck. How humiliating is that?

By the way, did you know that you do not have to take harassing and humiliating phone calls from bill collectors? You don't. A lot of creditors use outside bill collection services to try to collect money owed to them. They know that the best way to get paid is to get the debtor to pay. It seems obvious. What the creditors and bill collectors count on is that you will be ashamed, guilty, and intimidated enough and will be ignorant of your rights as a consumer.

Some creditors will use a fake name from inside their own company because they know that the word "collection" seems more fear provoking than having someone from their company pleading with you to pay. They usually only do this when a debt is fairly new because they think they have a chance of getting it paid.

You don't want to forget that paying your debt is a good thing. People typically do not set out to incur debt with absolutely no intention of paying. This is why collection agencies rely on a person's sense of guilt or responsibility to pay even though they do not have any legal right to enforce the collection. The only way a collection can be enforced is to have the original creditor file some kind of lawsuit. The only way collection agencies can collect from you is to notify you by mail or by phone within certain parameters and convince you to pay. They can't legally harass you; they can't plaster your picture throughout town as America's most wanted for nonpayment of a bill; they can't threaten you with bodily harm.

## Dealing with Collectors

Collectors for agencies have thankless jobs. Many of them work under aliases. Part of their strategy in collection is to act like such weasels that no one would want to be friends with them. The only way they get paid is by commission based on personal performance. They typically have a very low base wage and count on how much money they collect for commissions.

The main tools available to the collectors are letters and telephone calls. You can imagine that after a while when they get nowhere with people that they could get a little carried away.

The first letters are probably nice. They sound like reminders and do not include ultimatums. Then they progress according to how the person responds. They hope the recipient will be frightened of the veiled implications of impending doom and will call or respond with payment or at least a plan for payment.

If there is no response, they will typically follow up with another letter of a more demanding tone. If they receive no response after several more letters, they will resort to the telephone.

Did you know that phone calls by collectors can only be made to you between 8 A.M. and 9 P.M. They can't call you at work if they know your boss doesn't approve. They can't lie to you when they call by implying that your nonpayment is a crime, they must identify themselves to you on the phone, and they can't harass you or abuse you.

Donna, a woman who had been juggling her bills for a while, had tried to be nice when she got calls from creditors. She had not felt intimidated even after repeated phone calls from one collector because he seemed very reasonable and willing to work with her. She had gotten some dental work done and she had told the dentist up front that she couldn't afford it.

The dental office insisted they could work with her and that if she didn't have it done, the rest of her teeth could fall out so she relented. Spending $3,000, she knew it would take a very long time for her to pay it off and they agreed for her to make payments and to see if she could pay larger amounts from her bonus. She made what payments she could, but they demanded full payment one day without explanation. They said that she owed the money and would have to pay or the bill would be sent for collection. She was frustrated that she had only a verbal agreement because there was nothing she could do to prove to them that she had a plan to pay in small amounts each month. Because she never got a bonus, that was all she could do. When she had to start making smaller payments and skipped a month, the phone calls started again.

Meanwhile, one of the teeth they fixed fell out. This just added to her frustration and lack of motivation to pay the bill so she put it on the bottom of her list. Now the collector wasn't being so nice. He called all of the time to remind her she had agreed to a bigger amount. She said she couldn't pay it and would pay what she could.

She tried her best but the last straw was when he called and asked her why she didn't get a better job or a second job. She was floored and didn't believe what she had heard. "That isn't any of your business," she replied.

"Well you owe this big bill. Don't you think you should pay it?" Without even realizing he wasn't allowed to humiliate or harass her like that, she lost her temper and said, "I don't want you calling any more! You have no right to speak to me that way."

She then checked into her rights and wrote a letter to the collection agency telling them to stop calling her altogether about the bill. Now their only recourse was to contact her only when the creditor had initiated some kind of legal action.

## YOU HAVE RIGHTS

Consumers do have rights. The Fair Debt Collection Practices Act (FDCPA) clearly states that it was enacted because abusive debt collection practices contribute to a number of personal bankruptcies, marital instability, the loss of jobs, and invasions of individual privacy. The FDCPA was enacted in 1996 to protect individuals from all debt collectors.

Don't feel compelled to engage collection agents in a conversation when they call you. It is a waste of your time to try to explain to them why it is that you can't pay them now, how bad you feel about it, and how you'll pay them someday. They don't care. Their job is to intimidate you and/or lay a guilt trip on you. You should know that you can request that a creditor not call you again and, under federal law, that creditor should not contact you for at least two weeks, unless he has a specific item of information to impart to you, for example, that he has sued you. You should request any such information in writing.

The FDCPA is not intended to put collectors at a disadvantage, but before it was enacted there was all kinds of abuse toward consumers. Collectors would make false representations, harass people at home and at work at all hours of the day and night, and would use other kinds of intimidation tactics. The FDCPA has encouraged a more dignified system of debt collection. Most debtors want to pay their obligations. Collection agencies can have debts reflected in credit reports. Credit counseling is to the advantage of creditors because there is a high likelihood of repayment if debtors feel less pressured and are given a clear and rational way out from under the quagmire of debt.

If you are harassed by a collection agent or a creditor, contact your state attorney general's office of consumer affairs. If you can prove that the collection agent has violated the FDCPA, you may have grounds for a civil action against them. Either way you will aggravate them as much as they try to aggravate you.

Remember as you go through the process of bankruptcy that the FDCPA exists to spare people in financial distress further humiliation and disgrace. Bankruptcy is solution oriented. You have rights and you have responsibilities. This process will give you a balance between the two.

# 3 | Pre-Bankruptcy Planning and Asset Protection

Now that you have been through credit counseling, have looked into second mortgages, have looked into pawning your children—just kidding—you have decided that your best option is to file for bankruptcy. We see in the next chapter how to choose your particular method of filing—Chapter 7, Chapter 11, or Chapter 13, but for now we consider what you can do to strategically prepare for the process.

There are basically two kinds of debt: secured and unsecured. Secured debt is credit that has been extended to you on the basis of the value of the property purchased.

A nonpurchase money-secured debt is one on which you have borrowed money and put up other collateral, such as a paid-off car, as security to ensure repayment of the debt. A creditor holding a security interest in your property has the right to take the property in the event that you default on your payments. Often, if the property is no longer of sufficient value to cover the debt, you will be personally sued for the deficiency. In bankruptcy, you can discharge the deficiency, but the property itself will go to the creditor, unless you redeem it (pay an often reduced amount to own it outright) or reaffirm the debt (agree to pay for it over time, but often at a reduced interest rate and with a reduced balance).

Unsecured debt is credit that has been extended to you only on your promise to repay it. Most unsecured debt is credit card debt, although, for example, in the case of a new car, the minute you drive it off the lot the value of the car drops significantly, therefore, a portion of the new car loan becomes unsecured. A creditor with unsecured debt balances has no recourse other than to sue you for default and obtain a judgment against you, thereby becoming a judgment creditor with the ability to force the sale of your assets, place a lien on your house, force you to show up for a debtor's examination where he can question you as to the whereabouts of your assets, attach your business, your bank accounts, garnish your wages, and generally wreak havoc on your financial life in order to collect on the balance owed him.

Doesn't this sound like fun? You know you can't pay all or most of these debts. You are no longer in denial. You have sought help and, at this point, you have most likely done all you can to change your circumstances. You have gone to counseling and have pared down your standard of living as much as possible without having to pawn your underwear. So now, you are planning to file bankruptcy and you want to do all that you can to get prepared. You might still have some possessions with value that you want to retain, if possible. You know that creditors will want to get their hands on anything you have that is worth anything. If you file for a liquidation bankruptcy, you are going to lose anything that can be sold to pay off your creditors. So what can you do to prepare?

## PREPARING FOR BANKRUPTCY

The first thing you do *not* want to do is to hide assets like jewelry and other valuables. Don't "give them away to your sister" for safekeeping. Don't transfer any assets that can be transferred back to you after the completion of your case. When you sign the papers that will be used to support your bankruptcy filing, you will be making an oath that everything that you have listed is a *truthful* listing of your property. When you are in the court proceeding, you will be under oath that what you are saying is true. Aside from how you should feel about it, courts do not like it when people lie to them. You may not get caught, but you just might. *It is not worth it.*

In any bankruptcy, even a complete Chapter 7 liquidation, you will not be expected to give up *everything* you own. There are certain exemptions, property that is not in the parameters of what can be taken to satisfy your creditors. The types and amounts of exemptions vary from state to state, but they are intended for you to maintain enough to be able to have a fresh start. Bankruptcy law is not set up to be completely heartless. The trustee is not going to sell your child's special blanket or your sentimental photograph albums. The trustee is looking for things of a certain value that can be liquidated to offset what you owe so that your remaining debt can be legally and forever wiped out.

Another thing you do *not* want to do is charge many items on your credit cards right before you file with the knowledge that you are going to try to have that debt wiped out. Even though it may not seem so, it is essentially theft. Everything you do in the year prior to your filing and especially within the previous 90 days to your filing is going to be scrutinized closely by the court. Avoid the temptation to have that last little shopping spree.

## TAKE INVENTORY

One of the things you might want to do before taking direct steps toward filing is to take an inventory of your belongings. You don't need to know every little thing, because if you are like most of us and are a true reflection of the product of your consumer debt, you probably have too many odds and ends to enumerate. What you want to do is inventory anything that appears to have value. You will not want to think in terms of replacement value but of what it could bring in an auction, yard sale, or through a liquidator. You can bring in some experts for estimates but be aware that appraisals may cost money.

What you will find, if you haven't already tried to liquidate certain items to pay bills, is that most personal property will never bring close to what you paid for it. Even at auction, the buyers are looking for bargains and will likely get them. If, however, you have many things of tangible value, you will want to consider selling them before you file so that you can use this money to reduce your bankruptcy estate. There may be debts that are secured and therefore not dischargeable in bankruptcy. You are going to be stuck paying them no matter what. These debts include the mortgage, the IRS, and other collateralized loans.

If these are debts that you are going to have to keep or ones that you hope to reaffirm, such as a car or the house, you can pay the value of your liquidated assets toward what you owe on those items.

This is better than having the trustee liquidate all of your assets of any value to pay off debts that will be wiped out in the bankruptcy. You are in dire straights. You have to do everything you can to keep yourself afloat. Although you might feel a great deal of guilt over not being able to pay your creditors, get over it. You are now in survival mode. Defer your guilt to a time when you can afford it.

## EXEMPTIONS TO PRE-BANKRUPTCY PLANNING

There are some exemptions that are relevant to your pre-bankruptcy planning. While you can't legally squirrel away your valuables, you can sell certain items and use the funds to pay down some of the value of your exempt property. One of the most common forms of pre-bankruptcy planning is to use liquid assets, meaning things you can sell, to pay toward the equity of a home.

If your state has a liberal homestead exemption, it will be very helpful to you to pay down the equity. Each state is going to give you a dollar amount that you are able to keep out of the equity of your home so you can have something from which to build your new life.

Equity is defined as the difference between what your property is worth and what you owe on it. The worth of your property will be determine by such factors as appraised value and what someone would pay for it in the current market.

More specifically, equity is the difference between what your property is currently worth, that is, what it would sell for in the market today, often referred to as its "fair market value," and what you owe on it, if anything. For example, if houses like yours in your neighborhood are currently selling for $150,000 and your mortgage balance is $75,000, your equity in your home is $75,000. Likewise, if your automobile would bring $10,000 if you put it in the local *Car Trader* and sold it and the outstanding balance on your auto loan is $8,000, then your equity is $2,000.

If or when enacted, the bankruptcy reform legislation will set a federal limit on the maximum that each state can grant under their individual homestead exemption law—the figure currently proposed is $125,000. At the time of this writing, the states vary significantly in the protection afforded homeowners: In five states, the homestead exemption is virtually unlimited. A current bankruptcy legend has it that a certain Enron executive moved to Florida (where all of the equity in his home would be "sheltered") to build a multimillion dollar home so that he could keep his ill-gotten gains.

At least at this time, Florida is a debtor's haven because you can buy an expensive home there and have all of the equity protected. If this executive goes through a liquidation bankruptcy he can keep the house. If anyone wants to get at it, they can't. You can see why creditors, particularly credit card companies, might want to have a cap on the homestead exemption.

In states such as Alabama, only the first $5,000 of equity in your home is sheltered. So, if you are a wealthy debtor who wants to avoid losing everything, your pre-bankruptcy planning could include a move to Florida or Texas, another debtor's haven. You would then buy a lovely and expensive home and liquidate all of your nonexempt assets and property, which typically means anything of value that can be sold to satisfy your debts and pay toward your home equity. You can always replace your things, which will likely be liquidated in a bankruptcy, but you would not be able to replace their value that is now tied up in your lavish home.

If you plan ahead, you can protect your assets while sitting comfortably by the ocean or your swimming pool. You may need to find other ways to shelter your income should the proposed reform become law, but someone will always be crafty enough to figure something out. Who knows what creative ways debtors will find to strategically and legally plan to maintain the maximum amount of their assets in the wake of bankruptcy?

## LEGALLY SHELTERING ASSETS

When you plan ahead by sheltering your liquid assets within your home equity, you are maintaining as much of the value of your personal property as possible. The good news is that much of your property can't be taken either to satisfy a judgment or to pay creditors in a bankruptcy filing.

There are many things you can do that are perfectly legitimate that can maximize the status of your financial life when you finish the process of bankruptcy. You need to be creative and you need to know what is available. Not everyone is going to buy a big expensive house in a place with unlimited homestead exemption. Obviously, if you can do that, you are probably not going to be relying on this book because you will have at least 10 lawyers and accountants advising you at every turn. What is interesting for the rest of us is that this strategy is available in each state and for each person according to the limit of the home exemption. We have listed the exemptions as they exist currently from state to state at the end of this book.

Some states only allow an exemption of $5,000 for your home. This means that according to the state's homestead exemption, up to $5,000 of your home cannot be taken to pay creditors in your bankruptcy filing.

Here's another warning about being honest. You can do many things to prepare for bankruptcy in the year or even months prior to filing. Keep in mind, however, that everything you do that previous year is going to be scrutinized. If you suddenly start doing things that are completely out of character, you will raise many red flags. If you do anything that can be found to be a purposeful effort on your part to perpetuate fraud against any of your creditors, you can get into big trouble. If anything is found to be tainted, your entire filing could be reversed. Your trustee can disallow anything that doesn't appear to be above board.

So, if something smells bad even though you may not readily know why, it is not worth the risk. You want the full benefit of what bankruptcy protection allows. You have major debt hanging over your head and you want to be free of it. Your possessions, while significant to you, are not worth the repercussions of fraud.

By the way, you can't just decide to pay off some debts right before filing for bankruptcy. If you pay off certain bills in their entirety, such as your friend the doctor, while not paying anything to other creditors right before filing, it is called *preferential treatment*. Other creditors can say "That is not fair. You treated him better than me." This kind of transaction will very likely be disallowed and your other transactions scrutinized under a microscope.

Here are some things that are perfectly legitimate to do in preparation for your bankruptcy filing:

- You can use your liquid assets, the things you can sell, to pay off debts such as taxes. In fact, the bankruptcy people and the IRS confer all of the time.

- You can pay down your mortgage in those states with unlimited or significantly large homestead exemptions.

- You can take a cash advance on a credit card to pay your living expenses or your attorney if its more than 60 days prior to filing or less than 60 days if it is under the amount of $1075. There is probably a reason for that very specific amount but we just don't know what it is. If and when the bankruptcy reform is enacted, this will be changed to 90 days and $750.

- You can pay off credit cards having small balances so that you can keep at least one credit card for emergencies. It is most likely that a major credit card company will cancel your card anyway.
- You can liquidate nonexempt items such as a boat if you are behind in your mortgage and want to reinstate it.
- You can make your annual contribution to your IRA if you have one, or if you have any other exempt pension plans. Now you see why IRAs are good things to have.

    An exempt pension plan is one covered by the federal ERISA laws, or if not, it is one that is covered by your state's exemption list or the federal nonbankruptcy exemption list. You will have to check with your plan administrator or an attorney to find out about this.

- You can take out life insurance. Now don't get any ideas. The courts will look closely if your spouse is taking it out on you or vice versa and one of you mysteriously disappears. In this case, of course, you will have more problems than bankruptcy to contend with.

## SMOOTHING YOUR OWN PATH

When you know that you are going to apply for bankruptcy, you may not have the motivation to scramble every month to make payments on your bills. If you have a car, and you owe more than you own, you might want to simply anticipate what will happen and hand it back to your car finance company. Why wait for the repo man? You can legally own a vehicle with a book value below the amount of exemption. It may not be the style to which you were accustomed, but if it does not insult your sensibilities, it will be a debt you do not have to reinstate and you can wipe it out altogether.

If you have a car repossessed, you still essentially owe the remainder of the purchase contract. This is why the car company has an interest in the car. If you default, they get the car back just like in the situation of the house. If you do not want to keep paying on the car, your remaining debt will be wiped out in the bankruptcy procedure. This is presuming that you are filing for a complete liquidation.

For example, one couple, we'll call them Fred and Ethel, got married and didn't plan how they were going to manage money as a team. They both had been self-supporting and had never had to be concerned about someone else's spending. One of the first things they did when they got married was get his and her dream cars. They looked at the individual payments per month and said, "Oh, that doesn't seem so bad." But they had no thought about future planning or unexpected financial emergencies.

What is worse is that Ethel had a perfectly nice older car, that wasn't as cool as the beautiful SUV she eyed covetously, but it hardly had a mud stain on the rug. Fred and Ethel were in love and they had cars in their eyes. They got a pretty good deal on the first car, a beautiful black muscle car for him. Then they bought the SUV by trading in her car. The negotiations went well and they bought the car and were happy until they realized how much they lost in the deal by trading in a car that had "upside down" equity. They wound up owing far more than they expected because of their impatience and financial ignorance. "It seemed like such a good idea at the time," they lamented as they turned in the keys.

What happened is that their separate businesses—they were both self-employed—had taken a nosedive that particular year. In addition, they were essentially the blind leading the blind. They did not plan. When they had money, they would spend it, and when they didn't, they wouldn't. They had plenty of credit and were on an endless honeymoon.

When the bottom dropped out, they were both relieved to simply hand in the cars. They decided they would be satisfied with simpler cars in the future or at least wait until they had a more steady income and a long-range plan for their spending before they would ever consider another fancy car.

So what happens if you lose your cars? They did some pre-bankruptcy planning. Within the year before filing, they bought two modest cars in cash that were both below the value of the allowable exemption for a car. They were able to keep the two modest "junkers" for basic transportation and were given a reprieve until they could get back into shape to see what they wanted to do. They actually grew to love their used cars. They took better care of them than they had their fancier cars because they were so happy to have something to drive that wasn't going to give them daily anxiety.

Here's another story: George was living under a mountain of debt for years and had had enough. He was a nervous wreck and could not get ahead. He had wealthy parents, had never learned to manage money, and had always used credit to extend his means to have the lifestyle he wanted. Each year George's parents gave him a gift of $10,000. This was the maximum gift that a person could give to another tax free. (Now the amount is $11,000.) In addition, the gift has the ultimate effect of reducing the estate of the gift giver.

George was so tired of the pressure of debt that he became a minimalist. He liquidated most of his property, found an affordable apartment instead of the house he had been living in, and decided to free himself of his debt altogether. Even though he waited anxiously for his annual gift, which he had been using to stave off creditors, George decided to give his $10,000 to the bankruptcy trustee and received a complete Chapter 7 discharge. He walked away debt free and from that time forward could rebuild his lifestyle and use his annual gift however he wanted.

Even though George still welcomed his annual gift, he felt better about himself. He had always felt anxious and inadequate because he was never getting ahead and had even had to ask his parents for additional help beyond what they were already giving him. Many times, the inability to manage money is a direct result of living beyond your means with constant subsidy from prosperous parents. It is not uncommon in this generation for many adults to receive funds for essentials from well-meaning parents who want to help their adult children maintain the lifestyle of their youth.

The economy and cost of living differs greatly today as compared to previous generations and there is far more reliance on credit than ever before. Bankruptcy was not nearly as common 20 or 30 years ago as it is today. There are far more goods and services to buy today than ever. In this situation, George was not only freed from debt, he was freed from financial dependence. He learned the hard lesson of living within his means. Even though George was an adult in his thirties, he had never known exactly what he had available and how much he would need to spend each month to maintain a reasonable lifestyle. George was much happier living on a cash basis.

## WHAT CAN YOU KEEP?

Now that you know some strategies to use when getting ready to file bankruptcy, you will need to look carefully at the inventory we discussed at the beginning of this chapter to see what you can sell or what you simply can't bear to part with. Once you do this, you can determine how you want to go about your pre-bankruptcy planning. You have to look at whether you can keep the possessions you wish in the bankruptcy or if you are going to face losing them.

Before you file bankruptcy, you want to make sure that the things you really want aren't vulnerable to being taken away by your creditors. You have to look at the kinds of debt that you have to see what things are at risk.

The more you are behind in your payments on things, the more you are going to be harassed by creditors. If you haven't filed for bankruptcy and haven't heard anything from creditors for a while, don't be fooled. They could be lurking, waiting to get you when you least expect it. But you are going to be prepared. You are not going to wait so long with your hands over your eyes that your creditors are able to obtain judgments against you. You don't want creditors to gain control of you before you have a chance to be in relative control of yourself.

A *judgment* is a court order that says that you have to pay a certain amount to a creditor. This order has the authority of law behind it because a judge's approval gives the judgment holder the right to collect the amount from you. Once there is a judgment, there is no way for you to contest or argue against the amount owed. You need to pay attention to what is being sent to you in the mail. When finances are in disrepair, it is not unusual to throw bills into a big box or wastebasket and ignore them. It is easy to say, "I can't pay it so why bother." You want to maintain what leverage you have. You don't want other people, particularly creditors, to have too much power over you if it can be avoided.

A creditor obtains a judgment by suing you in court. If you show up at the hearing that will be held in civil court in the area where you are being sued, you can't get on the witness stand and simply say, "I can't pay it." You will need to prove either that you do not owe it or you will have to show that you have circumstances that would excuse you from paying it. When you go to court in a case like this, you can sometimes work something out with the creditor to make payments or to pay what you can. Your goal is to try to avoid allowing the creditor to get a judgment because then you are responsible for the full amount and judgments are not dischargeable in bankruptcy. Judgments are considered to have already been through the process of law.

Another way you can handle it is to not show up at your hearing at all. This happens often. In fact, the creditors count on this. They can pay their lawyers less and it is clean and easy to set the collection wheels in motion. If you don't show up, the court will issue an automatic judgment and this means that the creditor has the right to collect from you.

There are many ways a creditor can collect a judgment from you. A judgment can be used to garnish your wages, which means that a proportional amount of your wages can be directly taken out of your paycheck each week until the debt is satisfied. That certainly has some humiliation and lack of control associated with it. It is better avoided.

Your bank accounts can also be "attached" meaning that money can be taken out of your bank accounts to pay your debt without your agreement.

You can have a lien placed against your property. All of your creditors want to get paid and a lien means that if you sell your house, the person who holds the lien gets paid first before you get anything out of the sale.

When a creditor has a judgment, they can file a lien, which can force you to sell your property so the creditor can be paid. You don't always have the luxury of waiting until you want to sell. It is best to avoid a judgment lien against your house.

Judgments can be really problematic. A creditor can use a judgment to take your personal property from you. Creditors especially like things such as Rolex watches or other jewelry, things that conjure images of days of wealth gone by.

If you don't file for bankruptcy, are seriously behind in your payments, and have received a judgment against you, some of your assets may be liquidated to pay your creditors.

## STRATEGIES FOR KEEPING CERTAIN PROPERTY

If you are contemplating bankruptcy, there are some strategic steps the average debtor may choose to take to keep certain property. Keep in mind that if you do file for bankruptcy, all of your transactions within the year prior to filing will be subject to inquiry by the bankruptcy trustee and if found to be made to perpetrate a fraud on your creditors, they could be reversed. *Do not do anything fraudulent.* Although some people get away with it in the moment, there is always some kind of comeuppance.

Financial transactions that you make prior to bankruptcy that are outside your normal pattern of behavior could be considered fraudulent so make sure to document everything. Your actions may raise red flags but may be perfectly within your legal boundaries. Whether or not a trustee or judge raises an eyebrow depends on how far in advance you are doing it, as well as the specific circumstances surrounding your situation. This is just one more reason for obtaining expert legal advice. If you have even one objectionable transaction that is ultimately reversed, your entire bankruptcy case may be tainted and your discharge can be denied.

There are some additional strategic things a debtor can do to prepare for bankruptcy or avoid bankruptcy that under current bankruptcy laws will not constitute fraud. There are steps you can take that are perfectly legal and may serve your interests given your circumstances.

In states with generous homestead exemption provisions, you can reduce the amount of your unsecured debt by using some of the homestead exemption by refinancing your home to pay off your unsecured creditors.

The down side is that this is frequently the first bad choice made by debtors in the attempt to deal with unwieldy credit card balances. After maxing out the equity in their homes with second mortgages or equity loans, debtors all too often run up still more unsecured debt and end up in bankruptcy anyway. You are now stuck paying an unmanageable mortgage, which is not dischargeable if you intend to keep your home.

If you are going to run up more credit card debt, you may have your discharge denied if it appears that you had no expectation of being able to pay it back. For example, if you are unemployed or have defaulted on other debts, you don't paint a pretty picture to a bankruptcy trustee. It is understandable if you are really strapped and need to use your credit for basics or just to maintain some kind of living standard. However, if you are at this stage you should be preparing to file for bankruptcy.

## WHEN TO FILE

While you have some breathing room, you should file your case as soon as possible if you have the following factors:

- *You have an impending judgment against you.* This means someone has sued you and you really have no defense against the claim that you owe the money. In bankruptcy, not having the money is relevant, however, a suit against you for nonpayment can't be resolved in court in this way. Judgments can stay on public records virtually forever. It is very difficult to get them off your record although in some states you can accomplish this in the bankruptcy. In some states (where there is a specific statute for removing judgments), you have to file a certified copy of the discharge in every case where there is a judgment and ask the judge to remove the judgment.
- Your property has been seized (car repossessed, bank account attached, or wages garnished).

Alternatively, it might be advantageous to wait to file for bankruptcy if:

- Depending on your state and if your house is in foreclosure, you might want to wait because you may have a loan that would allow a reinstatement or forbearance plan.

  *Forbearance* is where you enter into a payment plan with the bank where the arrearages (past due balance) are added to the end of the loan, and you pay a higher monthly payment for a period of time after which the bank reinstates your mortgage. Like the satisfied debtor in our chapter on credit, this is a way to keep your home and perhaps work out a manageable payment. If you are otherwise solvent and have money coming in, you might be able to negotiate with other creditors to help you make it through. Sometimes they will even drop some finance charges or lower your interest rate. Keep in mind they want your business.
- You may want to sell your house and use the money to buy a more affordable house. It is better to do this by choice. You might even have some money to pay some creditors by making enough of a change in house price. At this point, you might very well welcome

the opportunity not to be house poor. Who needs something fancy when it is choking you?

One couple had a beautiful home in a lovely neighborhood but couldn't enjoy it because they knew that while they owed so much money and were in such debt they didn't really own it and could lose it. They sold their house, rented for a while until they could get back on their feet and now live in a modest home that is perfectly adequate. They enjoy it every day and know that it is not going to be taken away from them. It is wonderful to know that you can afford your lifestyle. Security can be far better than a large albatross with windows and doors.

## Face the Facts

Unfortunately, if you don't do something like sell your house or find a forbearance plan through your lender, you might not be able to prevent the foreclosure of your home. If this is the case, and you know you have learned the "don't need a fancy house" lesson, you should definitely consult an attorney who specializes in Chapter 13 filings. In Chapter 13, you can keep your home and create a payment plan for other creditors around it. You don't want to have your home sold on the courthouse steps. This is terribly disheartening. If you are brave enough to face your problems, you can prevent this. Be willing to act fast if you have to. Don't wait to seek advice.

Foreclosure sales happen because of the nature of a home mortgage and the legal ramifications of having one. When you take out a mortgage to buy your house, the bank has a secured interest in the house for the amount of the loan. A foreclosure action is a lawsuit where the bank asks a judge to give your house to them to sell so that they can recover the outstanding balance of the loan.

A sale on the courthouse steps refers to weekly auctions of properties that have been the subject of a foreclosure. The sale often takes place right in the lobby of your local courthouse, or sometimes, literally on the steps. At a sale on the courthouse steps, your home will probably be sold for far less than its fair market value. Investors will bid against the bank who may open with a bid as low as one hundred dollars. Investors may go up to and/or exceed the amount of the mortgage. You can't bid at your own foreclosure sale, since you were the one who defaulted on the mortgage, and besides the investor who buys the house has to come up with the cash the same day as the auction—if you had that kind of cash you wouldn't be in foreclosure in the first place. The bank has a credit for amount of the mortgage and if the investors fail to bid up to the amount of the mortgage, the bank gets the house and will then sell it in a foreclosure sale. If the bank buys the house and sells it and still has a deficiency (the sales price is less than the outstanding mortgage balance), they will sue you personally to recover the difference.

If someone else buys the property for more than the mortgage balance, and, if there are no other liens or second mortgages, it is possible that you would be able to claim the excess, but don't hold your breath. By the way, if you actually fail to properly claim it, it will eventually go back to the state.

## PROTECTING YOUR ASSETS TAKES TIME

You may want to convert some assets to exempt property, or you may choose to liquidate property and pay off creditors at a discount, rather than filing bankruptcy. However, if you go this route, you must be careful whom you pay because under the bankruptcy laws you might be making preferential transfers if you pay one creditor 100 percent and the rest nothing. If you liquidate, furthermore, you may owe taxes on the money received if it is more than what you paid for the item sold. For example, if you have restored an antique car that you purchased for $1,000 and sold it for $12,000, you'll owe income tax on $11,000. Keep in mind that the bankruptcy trustee and the IRS are on intimate terms: The trustee will report to the IRS if they find you've got a gain you haven't reported.

In choosing which strategies to take to protect your assets, you must keep an eye on what happens if you are forced to file despite your best efforts. The bankruptcy trustee has the power to do asset searches for real property and bank accounts, check for unclaimed cars with the Department of Motor Vehicles, make random asset checks, obtain your bank statements and canceled checks, and get your tax returns from the IRS to verify statements made on your petition regarding your income and property.

Because of the volume of bankruptcies filed, these checks are made randomly or only if the trustee sees a red flag in your filing. If you keep everything as clean and organized as possible, you should have little difficulty even if the hounds are after you.

Here are some possible red flags:

- Debts incurred for luxuries such jewelry, vacations, hobbies, and the like, within 40 days before filing.
- Cash advances over $1,000, within 20 days of filing. These will be presumed to be nondischargeable. Last minute buying sprees can taint your entire case with a suspicion of fraud. If you have taken cash advances, wait three months before you file.

The idea of red flags is important. If something sticks out so obviously, the trustee will exercise his or her rights to investigate your financial affairs to determine the veracity of your entire case.

The trustee gets paid a percentage of assets recovered that can legitimately be liquidated to pay off creditors. If your trustee puts you through a thorough investigation, this often includes requiring you to produce all of your bank statements for a period of time preceding the filing and can include a visit to your house to count your silverware! Once you file for bankruptcy, for the duration of the proceeding your nonexempt possessions are, in fact, under the trustee's legal control. You can't sell them or give them away.

Preparing for your bankruptcy filing is a very important part of your overall strategy. In fact, it is where you have the most control over the outcome of your case. In the next chapter, you find out how to compare your possible options for filing so you can make a decision with or without counsel about which type of bankruptcy would be most useful to your situation.

# 4

# Choosing Your Chapter

Now that you are over the fear and shame of filing bankruptcy and know a little about planning ahead and what types of property you can hope to hold onto after a bankruptcy, it is important to get a sense of what type of bankruptcy might be right for you. There are four categories of bankruptcy called *chapters*:

1. *Chapter 7:* A complete liquidation bankruptcy available under certain circumstances to people who have little or no assets, a mountain of debt, and no real way to pay for it.

2. *Chapter 13:* A reorganization bankruptcy that discharges some debts and, on agreement of a three- to five-year plan, allows a debtor to pay off debts without having to liquidate property to pay creditors. This chapter is for those who have an enormous amount of secured debt, such as house or car payments. If you have fallen hopelessly behind, filing under Chapter 13 can help you reorganize all of your debts so that you can hold on to your secured property. This chapter assumes that the debtor has steady income to support regular payments to the plan.

3. *Chapter 11:* A reorganization bankruptcy meant for businesses. Businesses have many different legal structures, which creates issues of the amount of responsibility the business owner has for the debts of the business or the amount of responsibility the separate entity of the business, if it is a corporation, has for the debt.

The intent of Chapter 11 is to allow the business to continue operating while giving it time to recover and become viable.

4. *Chapter 12:* A form of bankruptcy available to farm owners. This form is beyond the scope of this book.

## CHOOSING THE BEST OPTION

As you already know, you should look carefully to determine whether bankruptcy is your best or only option. Next, look at your income and debt circumstances to determine which bankruptcy chapter is available and best for you.

When you feel out of control, you can become so frustrated that you may want to put the keys to your house and car on your kitchen table and walk away. This is appropriate only if you have alternatives to housing and transportation; for most of us, that is rarely the case. You have to compare the type of debt you have to your income.

If you have been sued by one of your creditors and you have no defense other than you can't afford to pay the debt, you can assume that the creditor who is suing you will soon have a judgment against you for the amount of the debt plus his or her attorney's fees and costs. This judgment can be used to garnish your wages or your bank account, attach your assets, or place a judgment lien on your house. Depending on your state of residence and the exemptions that apply, a judgment lien may or may not be sufficient to force the sale of your house. In Florida, for example, a lien may be placed on your home, but regardless of the amount of the lien, the creditor cannot force you to sell your house. He or she must wait until you decide to sell or until you die. This is one of the reasons that debtors like Florida.

If you are behind in payments, are on the verge of having judgments against you, and can hold onto your mortgage only if you catch up on all of your debt, determine how much debt you can comfortably carry. If the answer is none, you need to consider Chapter 7 and should file as soon as you can finish your paperwork.

## DETERMINING HOW MUCH DEBT YOU CAN ACTUALLY CARRY

To help you make a decision, determine if your basic living expenses are about equal to, or more than, your income and whether most of your other assets are either exempt or exemptible. The amount of debt that you feel you can carry is a highly individual decision; for example, if your income is $1,250 a month and your basic living expenses are just about the same, a debt of $10,000 or even $8,000 is potentially insurmountable. The credit card company won't mind. You will be considered a good customer if you regularly pay your minimums at the exorbitant interest rates you are obligated to pay. If you are this much in debt with a modest monthly after-tax income, it is very likely that you can never completely pay off this debt during your natural lifetime.

On the other hand, as your income bracket goes up, the amount of debt that you are comfortable carrying may go up as well. The consideration should be not only "Can I manage to pay the minimum payments?" but also "If I pay the minimum payments, when, if ever, will I get this debt paid off?" If the answer seems to be never, you should consider bankruptcy. But, bankruptcy won't work for everyone. If you choose Chapter 7 liquidation, you will lose any nonexempt property of value to pay off your creditors.

To look more closely at how your income balances with your debt, compare your income with your expenses. The bankruptcy trustee looks at this, so you should, too. Calculate your monthly income and expenses to see a more accurate picture of your overall financial status, as follows:

- Determine your gross monthly salary.
- Subtract all employer deductions (social security, insurance, federal and state taxes, union dues, life insurance, etc.).

The result is net income. Next, calculate your basic living expenses including:

- Mortgage payment(s) or rent.
- Utilities.
- Insurance payments (house, health, life, car, disability).
- Food (include groceries and necessary eating out). Bankruptcy judges typically do not question this figure but be reasonable. Fancy restaurants are not a necessity.
- Monthly clothing expense (based on your annual estimate of new clothes bought).
- Cleaning.

- Magazines.
- Entertainment (a reasonable sum for an individual might be about $200 a month).
- Contributions to your church or synagogue (never more than 10 percent, and be prepared to prove it).

When you complete bankruptcy papers, you are making statements under oath; and if you are dishonest, you can be found guilty of perjury. This is very serious business; therefore, be careful to tell the truth. At the same time, reasonable estimates of how much you spend eating out or annual clothing expenditures don't have to be accurate to the penny. Don't underestimate to please anyone. Use reasonableness as your guideline; however, what is reasonable to you may not be reasonable for other people. Try to be objective and reasonable.

If you claim large losses from gambling in your bankruptcy filing, be prepared to prove it. There is a bankruptcy court legend about a famous comedian and notorious gambler who declared bankruptcy, claiming a big gambling loss—and brought in bags of old racetrack tickets to prove it. The judge went through the bags and threw out the tickets with shoe prints on them.

## CONSIDERATIONS FOR FILING

The basic considerations in choosing to file and under what chapter are the following:

- Your overall financial picture—compare income to expenses.
- Importance of keeping nonexempt assets.
- Your income from employment versus household, medical, and other expenses ratio, and the type of debt you hope to discharge.
- A second home or other real property such as a time share or other vacation home.
- Vehicle equity of significantly more than $1,000 (under the Florida exemption laws).
- Property in foreclosure.
- Potentially fraudulent transfers.
- Charges to creditors with no apparent ability to pay.
- Child support.

- School loans.
- IRS arrears you would like to discharge.

If you have more than two of the foregoing conditions as a prominent part of your financial picture, a Chapter 13 bankruptcy or filing may be the more appropriate route for you to take.

The most common bankruptcy, Chapter 7, is most suited if you have moderate to low income with few assets other than a home, a recently purchased new car (no equity), or a "junker" (very inexpensive) or leased vehicle, with an unsecured credit card balance as the majority of your debt and you are being sued by a creditor. Essentially, you should look for relief under Chapter 7 if you own little other than the property listed as exempt in your state (see Appendix C) and you are willing to give up your nonexempt property.

Even if your property is nonexempt, the trustee considers how difficult it would be to sell and what commission would be available to the trustee through the sale. Trustees sometimes abandon a valid interest in property with exempt value of $2,000 or 3,000. However, do not rely on luck that you fall in the "too much hassle" clause; be prepared for anything.

As emphasized earlier, if you want to have a smooth bankruptcy filing with the least amount of sweat, you should anticipate some red flags that will alert a trustee to closely scrutinize your case. You could be the most straightforward debtor on earth, but if there is any suspicion at all, your filing will drag on and be unpleasant or, worse, disallowed. Make no assumptions about this process. Although the procedure is black and white, there are many subjective factors involved, including the impressions of a trustee.

Red flags that trustees look for in Chapter 7 filings include:

- Extraordinarily high amount of credit card debt given your income.
- Any one creditor owed more than $10,000.
- Closing bank accounts or safe deposit boxes before filing.
- Transferring assets to relatives before filing.
- Ownership of expensive electronic equipment (or gift thereof to relatives).
- Ownership of musical instruments or exotic pets such as birds, monkeys, hunting dogs; that is, any personal property that may be of greater value than you have claimed.

Expert advice is advised if you suspect you fall into one of these categories.

If you are found to have too much "discretionary" or excess income over your basic living expenses, you can be denied on the perception of bad faith. Because everything is relative, make it clear in your filing why you seem to have the excess if in fact you do not have access to it. You must prove clearly why you cannot pay your bills.

## LEARN TO PRIORITIZE

After you have made up your mind to file for bankruptcy, or, if you are already delinquent or paying late on your bills, you may choose to stop paying all of your nonessential bills. You must also stop charging on your credit cards, and take no cash advances. Prioritize: If you can't pay all your bills, pay your car, housing, insurance, utilities, that is, the bills you need to pay to support yourself, support your family, and as needed for your employment.

## FILING CHAPTER 7

Even though you see merits in filing a Chapter 7 as a way out, it may not be an option. You cannot file for a Chapter 7 discharge if you have received a discharge in any form of bankruptcy within the past six years. The date runs from the date you filed, not the date you received the discharge.

In general, you cannot file if you have previously filed for bankruptcy and your case was dismissed within the past 180 days (in this case, you may want to file for a Chapter 13 bankruptcy, which has fewer restrictions). You may not want to file for bankruptcy if you have a cosigner whom you don't want to leave on the hook. In this case, you can either not file, or file but agree to repay that one debt only. If you think you may need to incur additional debt for necessities in the near future, you may want to delay filing for bankruptcy, but understand that borrowing money with no reasonable expectation of being able to pay can be considered fraud. Only debts incurred before filing for bankruptcy can be discharged. Debts incurred after filing are yours for keeps, or at least the next six years (eight years after the Reform Act of 2002 becomes effective).

Chapter 7 bankruptcy is the most commonly used method for individual debtors to get permanent relief from debt that they cannot afford to pay. The process usually takes from three to four months, but it can take longer, depending on the trustee (the luck of the draw) and whether a creditor objects (a result that you seek to avoid).

To begin your Chapter 7 case, you must complete about 20 pages of forms, listing, under penalties of perjury, all of your property, income from all sources, many of your property transactions for the past two years, living expenses and debts, and property that you claim to be exempt. If you choose to represent yourself, the only cost is the $200 filing fee.

At the time of filing, you will be assigned to a trustee and judge, and a meeting of creditors will be set. Most of the time, and if you get it right, the meeting of creditors is the only time you have to go to the courthouse after filing the papers. The trustee's job is to evaluate your case and process your paperwork with the primary duty to see that your creditors are paid as much as possible from your nonexempt assets. The trustee is motivated by more than integrity in this process: He or she gets a percentage of any assets recovered for your creditors.

If you have done your job right and appear to be honest, the trustee processes the paperwork without investigating your allegations, the creditors get nothing, and you walk away debt free and much wiser. Having obtained a discharge, you no longer have any legal obligation to pay your creditors. The court sets a hearing to officially discharge you, thus freeing your nonexempt property from the temporary legal bondage of the trustee. You do not attend this hearing; the discharge papers are mailed to you. You should retain all bankruptcy papers for life.

## FILING CHAPTER 13

The other option as an individual, married couple, or small business or sole proprietorship is Chapter 13. Chapter 13, which is more complicated and more expensive than Chapter 7, requires that you submit a repayment plan obligating you to repay creditors a portion of the total debt owed.

As a rule, a debtor chooses Chapter 13 only when there are nonexempt assets that he or she does not want liquidated to pay creditors and/or if income is significantly higher than basic living expenses (but not high enough to keep up with the debt payment). Under Chapter 13, a petition is filed as in Chapter 7; in addition, a plan showing how much you are going to pay your creditors over either a three- or five-year period of time is required. The amount of repayment is based on an estimate of future income. At the end of the three- or five-year period, any remaining balance due your creditors is wiped out.

During the course of the plan period, you remain under the jurisdiction of the court, which can either give you a break if you temporarily cannot keep up with your payment schedule and demand that you pay more if you are making more, or the court may feel you are living "too high on the hog" and should lower your expenses. Whenever possible, a Chapter 7 filing is preferable to a Chapter 13 because of the ongoing obligation to account to the court for years of your life. If you file under either Chapter 7 or Chapter 13 and discover that the other is more appropriate for you, usually you can convert your case to the appropriate chapter.

## FILING CHAPTER 11

Chapter 11, reorganization for businesses, is used less commonly by individuals with a great deal of assets and who do not qualify for Chapter 7 or Chapter 13. It can also be for wealthy individuals.

Owning your own business is a statement of the American dream. Many of us want to have the option of creating something and seeing it grow into something successful. On a basic level, we simply do not want to spend our lives punching a time clock while we see our hard labors used to make someone else wealthy.

Some of us are simply entrepreneurial in spirit. We can't stay within the parameters of any box and are not happy in anything that does not allow us room to grow. Some of us may be unemployable because we have such distaste for authority that we can't survive as a team player in any environment. Whatever the reason, many small businesses are an extension of someone's dream, which eventually becomes an entity.

Small businesses have unique challenges: From a business and monetary standpoint, there is often little or no distinction between the debts and assets of the business and the debts and assets of the business owner. You may have equipment and fixtures related to the business, but if you are a small business owner, you are likely to be personally liable for everything that requires your guarantee of payment.

When starting a small business, there are many considerations when choosing how to structure the entity. There are many opportunities to create your business in such a way as to limit your liability should your business take a turn for the worse. No one goes into any venture with the expectation of failing. However, any new business venture is a calculated risk, which brings with it the possibility of many things that may not work out to your satisfaction. In other words, many small businesses fail.

If you are a small business owner facing bankruptcy, you have many options. A comprehensive discussion of those options is beyond the scope of this book, which is aimed at the individual and sole proprietor who may be approaching bankruptcy without legal counsel or with only a paralegal. Those filing for Chapter 11 bankruptcy definitely should seek legal counsel because of the potential complexities involved.

A Chapter 11 filing is referred to as a *reorganization* and provides the debtor the ability to force creditors to accept reduced payments and stop collection actions while the business tries to get back on its feet.

Under Chapter 11, the debtor is required to submit a repayment plan that must be approved by a committee of creditors, who are entitled to have legal counsel of their own, but which is paid for under the repayment plan. Deciding whether a business should file a Chapter 7 bankruptcy in which the assets are liquidated and distributed among the creditors or file a much more complex and expensive Chapter 11 requires expert legal advice. Although we give you some basics about Chapter 11, you should consult an attorney and retain someone who is familiar with the process. When choosing a Chapter 11 attorney, find someone who understands business and is a good negotiator who can avoid litigation. You want to have someone who can find a way to satisfy your creditors while preserving your interests. On the other hand, you want someone who has experience with Chapter 11 and is not afraid of a fight if there is one. Many attorneys can do a basic bankruptcy. Chapter 11 is a specialty. Do not put the future of your business in the hands of someone who is not competent to handle the challenges that may arise.

## TAKE ADVANTAGE OF THE AUTOMATIC STAY

Regardless of which chapter you file, you have the advantage of the automatic stay, which is put into effect as of the date of filing the petition with the court. That means that all collection actions by your creditors must stop once they are notified that you have filed. In some specific instances, the stay can be lifted by the court if the creditor objects. For example, if you have failed to pay your rent, your landlord will be able to successfully ask the court to lift the stay and proceed with an eviction action. You must keep in mind that while bankruptcy can provide relief from debt, it is not a cure-all.

## THE BANKRUPTCY BACKLASH

So, what are your actual options? In our rush to unload the debt burden that seems to have been weighing us down for so long, we need to examine the consequences that each filing will bring. Bankruptcy brings some backlash, discomfort, and temporary changes in lifestyle:

- Filing for bankruptcy stays on your credit history for up to 10 years and makes it more difficult (but by no means impossible) to obtain credit in the immediate future, including car loans and home mortgages.
- Under a Chapter 7 discharge, you may have to give up your nonexempt property, which will be sold to pay your creditors.
- Under a Chapter 13, you may keep your nonexempt property, but you will be forced to pay your creditors the value of the equity you have in that property under your repayment plan as well as a percentage of your earnings, and your financial life will be subject to scrutiny by the court for three to five years, depending on which repayment plan period you choose.

In summary, you should consider bankruptcy as an alternative when:

- You frequently find yourself taking cash advances on your credit cards to pay your monthly bills without the ability to pay it back in full.

- You are carrying large balances on your cards and you can barely afford (or cannot afford) to pay the minimum on each of them.
- You have been sued by a creditor for nonpayment on a debt, which you can't afford to pay.
- Your home is in foreclosure.
- Your car was taken during the night by the repo man.
- The IRS or someone else is garnishing (taking money from) your paycheck.

If you have reached a point where there is no alternative for Chapter 7 bankruptcy, you are ready for a major "do over." Anyone has the potential to get in over his or her head. History has painted a bleak and punishing view of those who are unable to pay their debts, but our more enlightened society is set up so that there are mechanisms for people to get back on their feet. Our country was in part pioneered by debtors fleeing debtors' prisons in Europe. The United States bankruptcy laws were established on the principle that everyone (who meets certain criteria) deserves the fresh start that bankruptcy can provide.

## SOME RESTRICTIONS APPLY

Chapter 7 bankruptcy has certain time restrictions: You cannot file for a Chapter 7 discharge if you have received a discharge in bankruptcy within the past six years—the date runs from the date you filed, not the date you received the discharge. In general, you cannot file if you have previously filed for bankruptcy and your case was dismissed within the past 180 days (in this case, you may want to file for a Chapter 13 bankruptcy, which has fewer restrictions).

Having a cosigner you don't want to leave on the hook, as discussed previously, is another reason not to file for bankruptcy (see previous Filing Chapter 7 section discussion).

## BEFORE YOU MAKE A CHOICE . . .

You may choose to file in Chapter 13 when you can't file a Chapter 7 for one of the time-limiting reasons listed previously—those time limits do not currently apply to Chapter 13 filings, which can be filed at any time. After or if the expected reform becomes effective, you can expect to see some limits placed on Chapter 13 filings as well.

You may choose to file under Chapter 13 if you have secured exempt property (such as a home in foreclosure) and certain nonexempt property that you wish to retain, and you wish to restructure your debt so that your payments become more manageable. Through a Chapter 13 plan, you can spread your payments over a three- to five-year time span as well as discharge a portion of your debt at the end of the plan period. The payment plan you and your attorney devise will be subject to approval by your creditors, who may try to force you to create a plan under which they get more or get paid faster.

But, because you are required to put only 90 percent of your excess income into the plan and your secured creditors, such as the mortgage holder on your home, are entitled to 100 percent of arrears and payments, your unsecured creditors have a right only to what is left after you pay your secured creditors pro rata; that is, you pay each unsecured creditor the same percentage of the debt as the other unsecured creditors.

To determine an approximate amount to pay unsecured creditors, follow these steps:

1. Take your remaining disposable income (Schedule J) after subtracting necessary payments to secured creditors, and multiply the disposable income by 36 (for a three-year plan).
2. Add the amounts you owe unsecured creditors.
3. Divide the total owed to unsecured creditors (step 2) by the total amount of your disposable income after paying secured creditors (step 1). This gives you each creditor's pro rata share.
4. For each unsecured creditor balance, multiply by the result obtained in step 3.
5. Divide the answer obtained in step 4 by 36 to determine the pro rata share to be paid to each unsecured creditor.

Ultimately, the trustee and the judge will approve your plan, and this can be done (and is commonly done) over the objections of the creditors. If, in the course of living under your Chapter 13 plan, you discover that you cannot maintain the payments and the judge refuses to reduce your payment plan, you can convert to a Chapter 7, provided your creditors still get what they might have gotten had you filed under Chapter 7 (i.e., the value of your nonexempt property). However, converting to Chapter 7 might result in losing your home if you can't pay the arrears or work out a reinstatement plan with the bank.

## HOW MUCH WILL YOU HAVE TO PAY?

You, your attorney, the creditors, the trustee, and the judge will apply certain factors to determine how much you will be required to pay into a plan on a monthly basis. Your income from all sources is considered, including not only income from your job, but also other income. For example, if your mother or a roommate lives with you and contributes a few hundred dollars a month to the household expenses, that is considered income as well. If you lose your roommate, it might very well mean you could fail to complete the plan and be forced into a Chapter 7.

Under your plan, you must pay at least 90 percent of disposable income into the plan and none into your retirement plan or savings account during the plan period. In determining your allowable deductions from your income, you are allowed the basic costs of living, including housing, utilities, insurance, child care, transportation, food, medicine, clothing, and the like (see Schedule J—Current Expenditures of Individual Debtor). Under the current law, these expenses are based on actual costs of living. Under the proposed reform, these expenses will be based on median costs of living in your region of the country as determined by the IRS. If, after making these deductions, you don't have sufficient excess money to repay your debts within the maximum period of 60 months, your only choice is to file for Chapter 7 bankruptcy.

During the plan period, if you must incur additional debt for a new roof or a new car, for example, you must ask the judge for permission, which is usually granted assuming your unsecured creditors still get the specified amount and you can pay off within maximum time permitted by law (60 months).

From a strategic point of view, when you and your attorney create your Chapter 13 plan, you should allow some flexibility within the plan period so that when the unexpected happens, and it always does, you can deal with it. First, don't give more than 90 percent of your disposable income into the plan initially, and make the plan as short as possible (three years). Therefore, when the inevitable new roof or new car dilemma arises, you have some wiggle room. Remember, length of time on your plan is somewhat flexible, from 36 months to 60 months. A 36-month plan is common if all you have is unsecured creditors such as credit cards, personal loans, and IRS obligations. But, more commonly in Chapter 13, debtors are faced with a sizable mortgage, arrearages, and credit card debt; therefore, 60 months is needed for the plan.

One of the down sides to waiting to file is that the arrearages become a huge nut to crack and threaten to bring the house of cards tumbling down should you be unable to complete the plan. Often, debtors find that they don't have sufficient disposable income to complete even a 60-month plan, and Chapter 7 is the only choice they have. In this situation, you will likely lose your house. You may want to consider selling your home while you still can.

## TRUSTEE FEES

The amount paid to the trustee varies in different areas of the country, with different methods of determining your plan payment. Some of the differences may be eliminated if the new bankruptcy reform laws are passed and come into effect. Currently, however, you may find a requirement for voluntary or mandatory wage deductions, and the trustee may require that you pay him or her not only the arrearage payment, but also your mortgage payment. In some regions, you will pay your normal monthly mortgage payments directly to the bank or mortgage company just as you always have.

Typically, your Chapter 13 plan includes any mortgage or other secured debt arrears, filing fees, the lender's attorneys' fees, late fees accrued before filing, the portion going to your unsecured creditors, and the remaining balance of your own attorney's fees.

One of the advantages of a Chapter 13 filing is *lien stripping:* If you have more than one mortgage on your house or liens on your house other than mortgages, for example, IRS liens, it may be possible to "strip off" or remove those liens to the extent that they exceed your equity in the house. It involves massive paperwork, but it can be done.

While Chapter 13 is designed to exempt property, if you own luxury items, you may have to convince the trustee that you should be allowed to keep them. Technically, you have to pay your unsecured creditors the same they would get if you had to liquidate your nonexempt assets in a Chapter 7 filing for distribution to your unsecured creditors. This is called the *liquidation test.* The liquidation test might require that you sacrifice your diamonds, yachts, and Rolexes unless you can pay off their liquidation value within the plan payment period.

Consultation with a seasoned Chapter 13 attorney is strongly advised to ensure that you create a livable payment plan and maximize the opportunity to create a "fresh start" for yourself. Those of us who have spent a great deal of time in bankruptcy hearings know that the debtor who goes it alone often runs into trouble at the plan confirmation hearing and can end up having his or her case dismissed. While some trustees are generous with debtors who attempt to navigate the judicial waters alone and may even offer advice, give the faltering debtor more time to comply, or even recruit an attorney from the audience to give impromptu advice, many are impatient and expect the debtor to be well prepared before entering the courtroom. In the same vein, we find that, all too often, Chapter 13 cases prepared by paralegals are also commonly dismissed. A paralegal may be familiar with completing the paperwork, but he or she is not a lawyer and is permitted only to complete the papers, not advise you on how the law applies in your case.

It is difficult, if not impossible, to give specific pointers on how the trustees in each state enforce the provisions of the code in a Chapter 13 filing. We have found that trustees vary in how they handle these matters, not only from state to state but also from region to region within a state. This is all the more reason for you to have a good, local bankruptcy attorney at your side.

No doubt the pending bankruptcy reform will bring changes to Chapter 13. We anticipate that its impact on debtors filing under 13 will depend on the region in which you reside. In some parts of the country, trustees have already incorporated many of the suggested changes as requirements under their own local rules. For example, in the Southern District of Florida, wage deductions are mandatory rather than voluntary, as they are in many parts of the country. Also, in the Southern District, a filer's entire mortgage payment, along with the rest of the plan amount, goes directly to the trustee for distribution. The most draconian measures found in the new reform package are expected to involve restrictions on who can file for Chapter 7 relief.

## LIFE GOES ON

The good news is that most debtors can live through and many can go on to live financially healthier lives. Typically, the newly bankrupt person is solicited for a new credit card shortly after his or her discharge—credit card companies know that after a discharge, a cardholder cannot file again for six years (eight after the reform goes into effect). He or she may even be actively solicited by car dealers and will, no doubt, in short order have a credit card, car, and checking account. It is not uncommon for people who have been through a bankruptcy to be able to close on a new house within two years of receiving their discharge. Remember to retain your bankruptcy papers for life. You will need them any time you apply for a loan. You, too, will live through your bankruptcy and restore your credit as you learn to live within your means.

## ASSESSING THE IMPLICATIONS

Before you make any decisions about filing for bankruptcy, you need to see what the implications will be for you personally and for the continuation of your business. If your business is doing reasonably well but is operating at a loss and not supporting your personal needs, you might want to seek ways to continue running the business while consolidating or seeking debt relief for your personal debts.

If your business is your sole means of producing income, the spirit of debt relief through bankruptcy is to give you the opportunity to keep it thriving so that you can turn it around. This is logical. If you are successful, you can pay your bills. It is as simple as that. Therefore, don't give up because you see that the money flowing out is not as much as your income. You may need to rethink how you operate your business just as you will rethink how to operate the business of running your home.

The small business owner has a tremendous challenge. If there were no dreams associated with small businesses, it is doubtful that any sane person would purposely subject himself or herself to the financial insecurity. Professionals such as lawyers, doctors, and dentists are considered small business owners; so if you are struggling trying to get your in-home printing business off the ground, remember that those who have struggled through years of education with the expectation of the large payoff are often struggling just as much as you are.

Small businesses require overhead incurred simply in the course of operation. There are licenses, office equipment, utilities, and open accounts to certain suppliers, as well as the need for insurance if you are to retain employees. No matter what your business, some expenditures will rely on your ability to pay a creditor the value of the goods and services. Sometimes setbacks are not enough to cause even a ripple in the potential for the venture. At other times, even a small problem can lead to financial disaster.

Of the many business structures available, it is not likely that you will be spared direct liability. As owner of the business, you sign contracts with suppliers just as if the business did not exist. The limited liability corporation (LLC) can protect you against certain things, but not every debt.

Running your own business is worth it if you can plan well. If you are sued for default on a debt and your business has no assets, the creditor is given a judgment against you, and can sue you personally because you signed on the dotted line. If you don't have many personal assets, which is most likely the case if you have been caught in the vortex of business demise, it is very likely that the creditor will attach your only asset—probably your house. If you then file bankruptcy and your state has a liberal home exemption, you will be excused from the judgment because the lien holder cannot take everything you have. The creditor might not be happy about this, but there is no recourse except to write off the debt.

## DEBT RELIEF

If your business is falling onto hard times, you can qualify for Chapter 7 debt relief. If there is no way to salvage the business and your personal situation is equally bleak, you can put everything, including all of your business debts, on your filing matrix. You may as well have it all under one roof. You are going to be starting over on all levels, so you need to consider changing your career as well as find a way to rebuild your personal assets.

Filing Chapter 7 to be relieved of your business debts does not mean you have to give up your business. The Chapter 7 debt relief allows you to keep certain assets needed for earning a living or running your business. If your assets fall within these parameters, you can truly start over and get back on your feet.

Chapter 11 bankruptcy is primarily used by businesses, corporations, and partnerships, and much less commonly by individuals with a great deal of assets (secured debts in excess of $350,000, more than $100,000 in unsecured debt, and the ability to repay a portion of it over a number of years) and who do not qualify for Chapter 7 or Chapter 13. A Chapter 11 filing is referred to as a *reorganization* and provides the debtor the ability to force creditors to accept reduced payments and stop collection actions while the business tries to get back on its feet. Under Chapter 11, the debtor is required to submit a repayment plan, which must be approved by a committee of creditors entitled to have legal counsel of their own, but which is paid for under the repayment plan.

Chapter 11 may be a good option for your small business, but it will cost you. Careful analysis is required before making this decision. Chapter 11 is a reorganization bankruptcy that assures (in the short term) that you can keep your business running while you rebuild and make efforts to push the business over the top out of the sea of red ink. Every business goes through a period of development where it must become profitable or fail.

In Chapter 11, the bankruptcy petition is filed, creditors cannot take away anything until the case goes through the bankruptcy process, and the business can be run for a period of time without the stress of creditors at the door. When a Chapter 11 petition is filed, the business owner is still in possession of the business and has the time to reorganize and pay creditors some or all of what is owed. The owner can work with creditors in a way that preserves his or her reputation. As we discussed in Chapter 1, confronting the problem is the best solution because the more you avoid the creditors, the more they consider it a personal affront.

## BUSINESS REORGANIZATION

If you are considering a business reorganization or Chapter 11 bankruptcy filing, you should consult with a law firm that specializes in such filings. Chapter 11 is expensive and, quite often, when all is said and done, fails to keep the business alive. Therefore, a careful assessment of the pros and cons of embarking on a Chapter 11 rather than liquidating under a Chapter 7 filing must be made with expert specialized advice. Deciding whether a business should simply go belly up and file a Chapter 7 bankruptcy in which the assets are liquidated and distributed among the creditors or file a much more complex and expensive Chapter 11 requires expert legal advice. Chapter 11, primarily designed for corporations and partnerships, is not discussed extensively in this book.

Chapter 12 is a business reorganization for small farmers and is subject to annual renewal by the legislature. If you fall into this category, you should obtain specialized legal advice in preparation for filing for relief under Chapter 12. While the principles remain the same, specifics on how to file under Chapter 12 are beyond the scope of this book.

# 5 It's Not Personal; It's Business

You're sitting by the barbecue with friends—people you can talk to. You share your frustrations about work, your stories about family, and your ideas for the future. Inevitably, one of you talks about the great idea you have for a business. It seems everyone wants to be in business for himself or herself. It is the American dream. It represents freedom from having to work for someone we probably do not like, being our own boss, bossing others, making our own hours, and the potential for making unlimited amounts of money.

We have all heard the stories of average people coming up with ideas that seem so obvious to everyone that we can't understand why we didn't think of them. We see that they take those ideas and turn them into some gazillion-dollar company. We are continually fascinated with television biographies or documentaries that show how simple people, through their own ideas and perspiration, have made it to the top.

Unfortunately, we also enjoy watching documentaries and biographies not only of their making it to the top with ungodly wealth, but also of their falling back into nothingness. We think it would never happen to us. Unfortunately, most small businesses do not make it off the ground; and if they do, they often cause the owner to lose his or her shirt. Many times, the person creating the business does not understand what it takes and how much work and capital investment is involved. In other situations, the business idea is simply something no one has already done because it is basically not a sound idea.

It is unlikely that you are dissuaded by the seeming odds against you, nor should you be. If you are willing to take risks and sweat it out, you may also have to live with the fact that your success may have ups and downs and many false starts. This is where bankruptcy comes in. If your business fails and you are unable to pay your debts, you have the same options available to you as any individual: You can file for bankruptcy. Your business structure will help you determine what chapter to file under, but you have the opportunity to get a fresh start either by a complete Chapter 7 liquidation, a Chapter 13 if you are a sole proprietor, or a reorganization bankruptcy under Chapter 11.

If you are a sole proprietorship or a partnership, you may be able to file under Chapter 13 because you are essentially your business, and your personal assets are at risk. Any business or individual can file for Chapter 7 complete liquidation bankruptcy. The type of business structure you have determines where the assets to be used to settle your debts come from. The result of Chapter 7 bankruptcy, regardless of structure, is that your business is completely out of business. It no longer exists. You will get a fresh start because you preserve personal assets according to the available exemptions. But you are getting a complete, fresh start for your business because there are no remaining assets.

On the other hand, a business can file for reorganization. This means that it can seek a way to pay debts, discharge some of the debt through an agreed-on plan through the bankruptcy court, and continue to operate during the period of bankruptcy. If a business owner wants to continue to exist beyond the bankruptcy, this is the way to do it.

## FOUR PRIMARY BUSINESS STRUCTURES

Four main business structures to choose from when you set up your own business are:

1. Sole proprietorship.
2. Partnership.

3. Corporation.
4. Limited liability corporation.

Determine what kind of business you are or how you want to structure the business you want to create. Although you want to be optimistic and believe that you will succeed, you need to anticipate that something can go wrong and that it is ultimately your responsibility. You need to decide how much liability you want to maintain and how vulnerable you want to be if the business should fail.

There are advantages and disadvantages to every structure. Certainly, there are no disadvantages to any of them if the business has continued success. There are more complications, for example, if you choose to set yourself up as a corporation, because there is a great deal of formality even beyond your initial filing. While you are a fledgling, there may be no real reason to incorporate. You can always change things when you grow large enough and want the advantages that a corporation can bring.

Whether you are better off starting as a sole proprietor or choosing one of the more complicated organizational structures such as a partnership, corporation, or limited liability company (LLC) usually depends on several factors, including the size and profitability of your business, how many people own it, and whether it entails liability risks not covered by insurance.

## SOLE PROPRIETORSHIP

To be a sole proprietorship, all you have to do is start a business. You can start selling jewelry, which will probably require some filing of papers to obtain a vendor's license. If you have a vendor's license you will be required to file a state sales tax return whether or not you sell anything. You can simply do consulting work and get paid for it. If you do something that you are paid for, you are a sole proprietor. For example, if you write and are paid for it or if you work on your own, you are considered a sole proprietor. You are self-employed.

If you want to generate leads or create a more sophisticated persona, you can create a fictitious name to call your company. You can register this name with your secretary of state's office if you think you might want to make it a trade name in the future. You can get a business account with a DBA (doing business as). You can have letterhead and business cards made. You are official.

The only way a sole proprietorship has any importance to you from a business standpoint is that you pay taxes as an individual and are held liable for any debts you incur in the name of your business. As a taxpayer, you must complete forms for self-employment tax so that you do not miss out on the pleasure of paying social security.

Small businesses in the form of sole proprietorship have unique challenges: From a business and monetary standpoint, there is often little or no distinction between the debts and assets of the business and the debts and assets of the business owner. You may have equipment and fixtures related to the business, but if you are a small business owner, you are likely to be personally liable on everything that requires your guarantee of payment.

## BEWARE THE PARTNERSHIP

If you work as a partner, share space, share ideas, share accounts, or share rent, you could be a partnership. You do not need to have a formal partnership agreement to be viewed as a legal entity that does have an impact on your life should you become insolvent.

Make sure you like and trust the person to whom you are joining your business troth or, at least, make sure he or she is savvy enough to make decisions that you can live with.

If you are in a partnership, your partner may acquire debt on behalf of the partnership without your consent unless you have a written agreement stating otherwise. If you write an agreement, you can anticipate all kinds of problems. You can make one partner in charge of business and financial decisions.

Keep in mind that no matter what planning you do ahead of time, both partners are liable for the debt of the partnership. Creditors do not view the partners as separate from the business, as in a sole proprietorship. If you default on debts that have a security interest, the equipment or item may be repossessed. If you have debt that is not secured, the creditor can sue for a judgment and the personal assets of both partners can be sought to pay off the amount, including your house, your car, or anything else of value you own.

If you go bankrupt, both partners are considered as establishing the basis of the bankruptcy estate for the purposes of the trustee. If one of you is more collectible than the other, one of you will not be happy and one of you is likely to flee the relationship.

## INCORPORATING

A more formal way to avoid direct liability for debt or lawsuits (which we do not deal with here) is to incorporate. You can create a corporation by filing papers, or *articles of incorporation,* with your state.

While you can do this yourself, it is advisable to engage an attorney to assist you. Corporations are regulated by state law; thus, there can be tax implications or other requirements about which you may be unaware.

The advantage to forming a corporation is that a corporation is considered its own entity as if it were a person. This means that debts or other liabilities belong to the corporation. This also means that taxes are paid by the corporation on profits; the corporation also receives the losses to be deducted from the corporate returns. The corporation needs officers and must hold periodic meetings.

A corporation as a separate "person" can make contracts and have debts. If the corporation defaults, the creditors cannot go after the assets of the owners of the business. You can visualize a veil over the corporation that separates the business from the personal.

The idea that there is less risk for the owner of the business if incorporated is very attractive to the entrepreneur, but it is often premature. When profits are low and the business is starting out, there is little or no advantage. The owner will have to guarantee much of the start-up debt to become established; therefore, the corporate separation might not have the intended protection. The individual is essentially a cosigner with the entity of the corporation.

## LIMITED LIABILITY CORPORATION

Another legal business entity is the limited liability corporation. It is a simpler structure than a corporation and serves to protect the owner from complete personal liability for the debts of the business. A filing is required for an LLC, but the burden of all the protocols of running a corporation is absent.

An LLC does not need a board of directors or meetings. An LLC is similar to a sole proprietorship and a partnership because the owner files a personal tax return with the profits and expenses of the business.

## REORGANIZATION BANKRUPTCY

If a business is falling on hard times and does not want to fail, the option of reorganization bankruptcy under Chapter 11 is a consideration. Chapter 11 allows the business to develop a repayment plan in which the creditors are able to participate on their own behalf until the court is satisfied that the plan is reasonable. The advantage of Chapter 11 is that the business can continue operating and can even incur new debt to maintain its health.

For businesses that are essentially the same as the individuals who run them, the Chapter 13 option is still available. If the business is small enough and is a sole proprietorship, Chapter 13, though not simple, is far simpler than Chapter 11. Chapter 11 definitely involves attorneys for each party and it can be difficult to reach agreement.

The advantage of the LLC is that the debts of the business are separate from the debts of the owner. The LLC in debt can't continue business operations. They are likely to liquidate and file under Chapter 7. Their assets are sold for cash by a court-appointed trustee. Administrative and legal expenses are paid first, and the remainder goes to creditors.

Secured creditors will have their collateral returned to them. If the company doesn't have enough money to repay them in full, they are grouped with other unsecured creditors for the rest of their claim. Bondholders and other unsecured creditors are notified of the Chapter 7 filing and should file a claim in case money remains for them to receive a payment.

Stockholders do not have to be notified of the Chapter 7 bankruptcy because they generally don't receive anything in return for their investment. But, in the unlikely event that creditors are paid in full, stockholders are notified and given an opportunity to file claims for anything left over.

If you want to set up a corporation, you must file papers with your state. If you set up a partnership, you are still personally responsible for any business debts. If the business acquires debts, even if they were originally incurred by the other partner on behalf of the partnership, you are still personally liable. If your partner doesn't have anything of value, the creditor can go after whatever assets you have. It is something to consider before you form a business alliance with someone.

## THE PLAN OF REORGANIZATION

The U.S. Trustee, the bankruptcy arm of the Justice Department, appoints one or more committees to represent the interests of creditors and stockholders in working with the company to develop a plan of reorganization to get out of debt.

The plan must be accepted by the creditors, bondholders, and stockholders and must be confirmed by the court. However, even if creditors or stockholders vote to reject the plan, the court can disregard the vote and still confirm the plan if it finds that the plan treats creditors and stockholders fairly.

### Advantages to a Chapter 13 Payment Plan

1.  You keep all your property, exempt and nonexempt.
2.  You have a longer time to pay the debt.
3.  The debts that are not canceled in a Chapter 7 discharge can be reduced in a Chapter 13 payment.
4.  You have protection against creditors' collection efforts and wage garnishment.
5.  Any cosigners are immune from creditors' efforts as long as the Chapter 13 plan provides for full payment.
6.  You have protection against foreclosure by the lender of your home.
7.  You can file a Chapter 13 after your Chapter 7 discharge to pay off any remaining liens.
8.  You can file repeatedly.
9.  You can separate your creditors by class. Different classes of creditors receive different percentages of payment. This enables you to treat debts where there is a codebtor involved on a basis different from debts incurred on your own.

### Disadvantages of a Chapter 13 Payment Plan

1.  You pay your debts out of disposable (post-bankruptcy) income. This ties up cash over the repayment period.

2. Some debts survive after bankruptcy is closed and you must continue paying.

3. Legal fees are higher because a Chapter 13 filing is more complex.

4. Your debt must be less than $1 million (e.g., unsecured debts are less than $250,000 and secured debts less than $750,000).

5. Your debt can linger for years, burdening future income. A voluntary bankruptcy is commenced when an individual debtor or a business files with the local bankruptcy court a voluntary bankruptcy petition, a schedule of assets and liabilities, and a statement of affairs.

Any individual, partnership, or corporation may file a voluntary bankruptcy petition under the Chapter 7 liquidation provisions of the Bankruptcy Act. In a liquidation, the bankruptcy trustee takes possession of all of the debtor's nonexempt property, which is sold for the benefit of the debtor's creditors.

## WHO CAN FILE CHAPTER 13?

Small business owners who have other income can file under Chapter 13. What is required is that you have a guaranteed source of income that is not based on the corporation. If your income is solely from the corporation, your remedy is Chapter 11, which is more complicated. Examples of businesses that can file under Chapter 13 are:

- Professionals who are incorporated because they are essentially their business.
- Solely owned corporations where there is income on the side from another job.
- Situations in which one spouse has income from another job. Any time the court can use income to substantiate payments to the court, a Chapter 13 could be applied.
- If there is a steady source of real estate investment income that can be used to support the payment plan.

There are many reasons a businessperson would prefer filing under Chapter 13 if bankruptcy is in the future. Chapter 13 costs much less overall. There are attorneys involved. In Chapter 13, the trustee takes only a small percentage of the assets of the company, and there is not an expensive legal process.

The disadvantage of a business filing Chapter 13 is that the debt has to be paid back almost immediately. In Chapter 13, the plan goes into effect within 30 days.

Although Chapter 11 is more complicated, there is a 120-day cooling-off period after the plan is filed, and no payments are required to anyone until the plan is approved, which can take from six to eight months. There is no payment on the debt for the business for all of that time; meanwhile, the business is still running and is able to begin getting on its feet.

Another advantage to Chapter 11 bankruptcy is you can discharge tax penalties that you cannot discharge in Chapter 13. Chapter 11 is a legal proceeding that typically ends in negotiated settlements. The two sides work to determine what is fair. The laws are only a piece of it. The outcome of the Chapter 11 depends on the quality of the negotiations and how the individual players deal with it. This is where a good attorney comes in.

## AVOID CHOICES THAT IMMOBILIZE YOUR BUSINESS

One of the biggest problem businesspeople have in Chapter 11 bankruptcy is that they are immobilized. This may seem like an anomaly for a person who was willing to take the risk to create a business. However, if it is your own business, there is a perception of failure and anxiety far beyond what people who can be objective feel. There are many layers of personal reactions to a business Chapter 11 filing.

If you are a small business owner, you need to stop feeling paralyzed by your own failure to pay back debt. No matter what you work out with your creditors, keeping the business going is always the better outcome. You can always liquidate. But to reorganize and keep it going helps you continue to build your dream. Entrepreneurs have to be prepared for the ups and downs. Many books have been written about the successes and failures of businesses. The success stories are very likely to have had some rough spots along the way.

Liquidation does not bring money to creditors. If you are so emotionally paralyzed, you can't work. You need to remember that you are doing something good for your creditors. You are not disreputable. You are courageous. Facing creditors to negotiate a repayment plan is a brave thing to do.

Another reason businesspeople become immobilized when faced with a Chapter 11 filing is that they worry they will never again get credit or no one will do business with them. This is the worst fear of the entrepreneur. It is tantamount to watching your dream go up in smoke.

The reality is that in the first days of the bankruptcy, suppliers or creditors will likely want cash. But you will typically be extended credit if you show you are doing better. Your suppliers or creditors want to continue to do business.

One businessman we know was insolvent, rock bottom, scraping all he could to pay anyone. After he went through Chapter 11 bankruptcy and rebuilt, he sold his business for a million dollars. He decided he liked the money more than the business, but he never would have had anything to sell if he had not been able to rebuild. He faced his problems and evaluated what got him into trouble.

There are many reasons a business goes out of control; typical pitfalls include:

- *Out of control costs:* Many entrepreneurs do not add this to the overall profit calculation.

- *Absentee ownership:* Be careful who is minding the store. Phoning in is not enough. Give up golf unless you are sure the business is solvent. Sometimes, business owners rely on staff to make decisions. If you are not supervising decisions of any consequence, you are bound to have problems. You cannot clone yourself no matter how good your employees and managers might be. Besides, they are spending your money.

- *Not researching and putting effort into finding new markets:* Other companies move ahead, and you are buried under the competition.

## MAKING THE DECISION TO FILE

As with any financially difficult situation, there are signs to consider in making the decision to file for bankruptcy:

- You are getting sealed letters from the IRS.

- You are afraid to open your bottom drawer because of all the registered letters.

- New suppliers ship only for cash because they know your reputation.

- Regular suppliers scream when they hear your name.
- You are using personal credit cards to pay business debts.
- You are using personal credit cards and cash advances, at 18 percent interest, to make the business payroll.
- You, the business owner, have not cashed your last three paychecks.

## AVOIDING FINANCIAL TRAPS

There are ways to structure and set up your business to avoid some of these financial traps. If you are a corporation or a limited liability corporation, be aware that your business is still a liability to you if you personally sign on the debts. Taxing bodies can pierce the corporate veil. If you personally guarantee liabilities, you are going to be sought after personally.

You can restructure your business to be a corporation and make sure it is capitalized so that the corporation can be party to the contracts with lenders or suppliers without having to sign personally. You must be capitalized sufficiently to be profitable. This is the law of doing business successfully. Always look at the big picture. Build slowly. Don't grow too fast without knowing that the money is coming in. As in your personal life, do not bite off more than you can chew and never spend ahead.

You will need at least your first couple of years to get to a solid base. Try not to outgrow yourself. Understand enough about accounting to read the critical information being presented. If you do not understand it, you will be insolvent. Business is not merely about selling things and making profits. The failed dot-coms didn't bother with issues such as revenues or profits. Business should not be about greed but about the bottom line to build the company to protect it from downturns. It is okay to want the bucks, but you need to be savvy as to how you get to them. Otherwise, you will be left in a puff of smoke at the creditors' hearing. Business is cyclical. There will be downturns, so be prepared.

Here are more reasons businesses can fail:

- Undercapitalizing.
- Failure of a large customer.
- Major dislocation in marketplace.

After the September 11, 2001, tragedy, many businesses failed. For example, the limo services at the airports had few, if any, customers. They literally had no business.

Other businesses affected by this event were:

- Airports.
- Travel agencies.
- Hospitality.
- Stores in lower Manhattan.

World events can have an unavoidable rippling effect; therefore, prepare for downturns. You may not survive, and in that case, filing Chapter 11 bankruptcy may be best. If there is a chance that the market will turn around again, this will allow you to keep the business open until the circumstances around you change.

## DO YOUR HOMEWORK

As in any bankruptcy process, preplanning is a must. What you do before your creditors' meeting is what will be the measure of your success. Research extensively and seek advice from someone experienced in the specialty area of Chapter 11.

Find the right attorney. Ask around or go into court and find other Chapter 11 filings that have been successful. Many bankruptcy lawyers handle only Chapters 13 and 7 cases. They take Chapter 11 cases even though they are not specialists in that area. A good Chapter 11 attorney has good communication with the client, listens, and answers questions. Businesspeople especially do not want lawyer condescension. You want a lawyer who will negotiate—not litigate.

You can actually go to court with stipulated agreements; in that case, you will not have to face motions and wait for the judge to decide. You have more control over the outcome because it has been negotiated ahead of time.

### Ways to Prepare
- Make sure you have enough cash to keep things going before you file for bankruptcy.
- Do not pay your unsecured creditors for a while.

- Make sure you have enough raw materials to use before you file to get you through the first couple of weeks or so and reject any executory contract by motion of the court.
- If you have long-term supply contracts, go to court to void those contracts.
- Get released from real estate leases or you can catch up the lease payments and renegotiate to stay in your present location. When you catch up the payments, you can often negotiate with the lessor to move you into less expensive space.

You are given the opportunity to scale down. This is a fresh start for your business. You can continue operating and pay off as much debt as possible.

## ERR ON THE CONSERVATIVE SIDE

As with any bankruptcy, the biggest problem businesspeople face is their mental state. They are sometimes no longer willing to make decisions. They don't trust their decision-making process and feel out of control. And most entrepreneurs are control freaks.

When you rebuild, always err on the conservative side, don't expand too quickly, don't chase business that is not profitable, and make sure the business is earning sufficient profit to go on, not necessarily a million-dollar business. Avoid getting into more debt. Don't borrow money. If you can't fund with the existing cash flow, you should not do it. Don't leverage the company until you are so far from the original problems that they are a distant memory.

# 6 Gathering Documents without Losing Your Mind

Whether you retain an attorney or gather your own documents to complete your forms, you will experience the bankruptcy phenomenon of document dysphoria. This uniquely high level of anxiety can lead to overeating, hair pulling, unexplained road rage, and all kinds of destructive behaviors. There are ways to diffuse this natural outgrowth of paper overload. The first way is to weed through the morass of documents before you even consider seeing an attorney or tackling the approximately 20 to 30 forms you must complete to file your case.

A basic list of the types of information you need to gather includes:

- A list of all creditors, including names, addresses, and account numbers of any credit cards you possess. You can find these on your statements or call the company.

- Credit card statements to see what you actually bought in case there are any discrepancies down the line.

- The deed to your house.

- Your mortgage papers, including the mortgage holder, address, and account number.

- A list of all secured debt.

- Names of any lien holders, including liens from judgment creditors and the IRS.

- Monthly payment statements and VIN number of your vehicle (typically found on a metal plate by your windshield).
- List of all assets (inventory) and a value you have attached to them. Remember, this is garage sale value and not replacement value.

Gather any other relevant bills or debts. Utility statements are helpful to establish your monthly expenses even though they are not part of the bankruptcy.

To begin your Chapter 7 bankruptcy case, you (or your attorney) must complete forms that request a list of all property, income from all sources, many of your property transactions for the past two years, living expenses and debts, and property that you claim to be exempt. These forms must have full disclosure to the best of your knowledge or you could be subject to the penalties of fraud. At minimum, your case will be dismissed. If you choose to do this without a lawyer (however, we don't recommend this), the only cost is the $200 filing fee. You can obtain the most current version of the forms online. However, after the Reform Act is resurrected, signed, and put into effect (180 days after it is passed into law), you can expect a big change in the existing forms and many new requirements (see Epilogue). Again, we strongly suggest you secure the services of a competent bankruptcy attorney, rather than attempting to navigate the uncertain waters of the bankruptcy court on your own. However, we provide some pointers in the next chapter that include a completed set of forms and specific suggestions. We have chosen the most relevant forms; however, your specific situation may necessitate additional forms. Unusual circumstances require legal advice.

Chapter 7 walks you through the forms and schedules required to complete your bankruptcy petition.

## LIMITS TO CHAPTER 7 BANKRUPTCY

Chapter 13 bankruptcy requires the development of a reorganization plan and different forms. The forms we describe here are for a straight Chapter 7 liquidation. You will not be able to file for Chapter 7 relief in the following instances:

- You obtained a discharge in bankruptcy under any chapter filed within the past six years (under the new reform laws, it will be eight years between filings).

- The court involuntarily dismissed your Chapter 7 bankruptcy case within the past 180 days (six months) because you violated a court order.

- You voluntarily asked for dismissal of your case after a creditor asked for the automatic stay to be lifted. (Debtors sometimes find it advantageous to file to stave off creditors' collection actions for a period of time by filing for bankruptcy and then voluntarily dismiss after buying themselves some time to regroup and avoid filing again.)

When you start your bankruptcy filing, you need only the information and documentation necessary to properly prepare your *petition for bankruptcy* (what the court calls your completed forms). More specifically, you need:

- *Credit card debt:* Name, account number, mailing address, approximate total amount of what you owe to each of your creditors. You must provide this information about every creditor, whether you want to discharge or retain the debt (more about this later). Usually, most of this information is on your latest credit card or loan statements.

- *Car loan:* Account number, balance, and address, even if you intend to keep the car.

- *Mortgage:* First, second, and so on, account numbers, balances, addresses, even if you intend to keep the house. (If you do intend to keep the car and house, you must keep paying the bills as they come due; a discharge in bankruptcy is a "fresh start," not a "free ride.")

- *Any other debt:* Current, handshake, verbal, contingent—you must include all of your debt, including a private loan based on a handshake.

Only those debts named in your petition will be discharged; therefore, if you omit someone, you cannot file again for six years. You may want to think twice about discharging medical bills if you are still under treatment by the billing physician. If you find yourself in this situation, you may want to delay your bankruptcy filing until treatment ends, or if that's not possible, find another doctor. As a last resort, retain the debt to the doctor (usually, you should retain only those debts for necessary items such as car and home). In spite of the tendency to want to hang onto just that one card with a $1,200 balance, you should take full advantage of the bankruptcy process and discharge all unnecessary debt.

## CONTINGENT DEBT

When you gather documents or ultimately complete the forms, determine whether you have any "contingent debt," debt that arises only on occurrence of a certain event. For example, if you cosigned a car loan for a friend, you should discharge it if you don't want to be responsible if the friend stops paying.

Did you personally guarantee any loans, security agreements, leases, equipment leases, and so on in connection with a business venture? If yes, those can come back to you when you least expect it. Don't leave any loose ends. Just when you least expect it, your wages could be garnished or your house liened and you could even be forced to sale in many states, just because of that little personal guarantee on a business obligation that went south and you forgot about it. So, think about all of your business ventures very thoroughly and be sure to consider them when you file. Other documents you need include:

- Your paycheck stubs and last couple of years of tax returns. This information provides your net monthly income after all deductions and the total amount you earned in the past two years from all sources.

- Information about all of your monthly expenses.

- A "guesstimate" of cost utilities, for example, an amount that represents an annualized monthly amount taking into account seasonal variations for heating/cooling. However, provide reasonable estimates that could, should it become necessary, be substantiated by your actual bills.

- Names, addresses, and account numbers of all banks in which you had accounts for the last two years, including safe deposit boxes.

- Case numbers and the information about any lawsuits against you.

- Case number and pertinent names for any litigation you have initiated.

- Information about expected increases or decreases to your income in the coming years.

- Information about any expected tax refund.

- Possibly, your last six months' worth of bank statements. If the trustee suspects something fishy or if you are the lucky random audit, you may be asked for bank information. So, even if you would never intentionally misstate your affairs, be sure that the income and expenses you declare are substantiated by your bank statements, or if not, have a reasonable explanation as to the discrepancy.

## CREATING A CREDITOR MATRIX

After gathering all of your documents, files, and stubs, you should create a *creditor matrix*—a four-line address for each creditor, which you can copy from the bill in most cases. This is required in every jurisdiction; most now want it on a disk. The bankruptcy office in your jurisdiction will provide a detailed explanation of what it wants and how, which makes it easy to notify your creditors that you have filed. It is important for the matrix to be correct; however, if you later find an error, you can file amendments to any of these papers, until after the discharge. Even then, you may be able to reopen the file to include an omitted creditor, if you can show that the creditor was not harmed by being left out the first filing. Usually, no harm is presumed in a *no assets* case; that is, a case where none of your creditors received anything. Creditors need the same notice so they can lay claim to the assets that are going to be liquidated by the trustee. The earlier claimants get first proceeds. If a creditor is not notified, it is at a marked disadvantage. This, of course, applies only to unsecured debt.

Whether you are filing your own bankruptcy or you are working with an attorney, the paperwork involved may feel daunting. If you have an attorney, all you really have to do is provide the information he or she requests as completely and promptly as possible. If you understand what it is you are preparing and why it is needed, it can become less of a headache and can, to some extent, help you feel that you actually know what is happening.

The process of bankruptcy can feel like wading in mud if you do it yourself. It can also feel like mud if you hire a competent attorney but do not understand what is happening around you. Ask questions. It is complicated only because of the amount of supporting documents required. When the documents are all pulled together to create an overall picture, it is apparent why they are needed and the process seems less confusing. Remember that bankruptcy is a very black and white process. Although there are nuances in how certain information is analyzed by the trustee and ultimately received by the judge, the numbers are the numbers.

Unless you are committing fraud (in which case, you are on your own as far as we are concerned), the information you confirm to be true to the best of your knowledge will be what is used to determine the outcome of your case. There may be questions on the part of the trustee, which need to be answered during the investigative stage of your case; however, there is no cosmic mystery as to what it is that you put on your paperwork.

One client ran a business and was filing personal bankruptcy. Under the circumstances, the man was going to be able to continue running his business so he could rebuild. The business had few assets except for the man's own labor. He was the business. However, the trustee wanted to see further what might have gone wrong and whether there were receivables—money that is owed to the company for services rendered—that would be adequate to satisfy the personal debt. As you know, if you have a small business, the two entities—you and the business—are not completely separate during the course of the bankruptcy. You directly owe business bills unless you are able to work them out to maintain the viability of the business.

In this case, because the business was essentially the labor and work of the owner of the business, the trustee looked at more documents to see if what he had been shown in the original filing was all there was. The trustee is looking to determine if there are any assets to add to the bankruptcy estate so they can be sold to pay off debts.

If you are filing the forms yourself, make sure what you have to do is simple. There are many do-it-yourself kits that promise to make things easy, but the issues involved can be more difficult than they seem. If there are any unclear issues with your case, you might find that you wind up hiring an attorney anyway when you determine that you don't really know what you are doing.

There are businesses that will complete forms for you, but they often charge a great deal; for the money spent, you might as well have someone in your corner who can take your case as far as it needs to go. Paralegals can only prepare the paperwork based on what you provide. Law forbids them from advising you about the law. Often, they do offer advice, and, just as often, their advice is dead wrong. One of the debtor-friendly sections of the Reform Act requires stringent disclosures by nonlawyer petition preparers as to their inability to advise debtors about the laws of bankruptcy.

## AVOID STRESS

Our main recommendation when it comes to the bankruptcy experience is to avoid as much stress as possible. When you are "penny wise and pound foolish," you save money that seems like a good idea at the time but, in the long run, can have unneeded repercussions. Even though your case goes along without a hitch, you still have to factor in the anxiety factor associated with completing forms that you don't really understand.

This is similar to using tax-filing services. In that situation, it is appropriate to rely on a service that can do the paperwork for you because there is no definite court appearance involved. People who prepare tax returns for other people and are compensated for it are required to certify that they have prepared the forms. They have the responsibility to correctly prepare your forms within the normal range of human error.

No certification is necessary for people who assist in the preparation of bankruptcy forms on your behalf. However, if you hire an attorney for about the same amount, including filing fees, for a simple bankruptcy, your attorney is held to a standard of practice that is intended to ensure that you are receiving competent advice.

If you are confident that you have simple forms and a simple case and do not become automatically glassy-eyed and nauseated when you see pieces of paper with lettering and empty spaces for information, be our guest. We hope to give you some insights into how to maneuver through the bankruptcy waters safely.

There are many opportunities for you to prepare your bankruptcy papers online. However, even if you use a computer program that enables you to easily complete the paperwork, you still must know how to respond. Most attorneys prepare bankruptcy petitions on software programs that generate the required schedules, but the trick isn't in the program that automatically does the math; the trick is in properly interpreting the law as it applies to your facts.

Consider the costs and promises as with anything else. One Web site claims to have the software that bankruptcy attorneys use to file their cases. The program may streamline the process of completing forms, but it does not substitute for knowing what to do with them. If the program is affordable, you might think it would be a useful thing to do before meeting with your attorney. It is, in most cases, actually redundant because your attorney will ask you for the original documents, stubs, and information anyway. The forms provided in this book and our explanations should help you see exactly what information is necessary to give your attorney and/or the bankruptcy trustee the complete picture of your finances at the moment you wish to file.

## PREPARATION IS EVERYTHING

The most important and useful thing you can do before meeting with an attorney or when sitting down to complete the forms yourself is to have everything available. Make a special file. Keep organized. If you have never been organized about anything else, make sure you make this a priority. If you are constantly trying to gather documents, you are making things confusing and stressful. The forms and information requested are carefully designed to reveal the big picture of your case.

When you are mentally preparing for bankruptcy, it is common to lump everything together. The paperwork process can be anxiety provoking because many of us keep lousy records. When you consult with your attorney, many of the forms can be completed right then. The best use of your time is to gather:

- All of the latest bills, including bills from third parties such as collection agencies and collection attorneys.
- Paperwork on lawsuits against you.
- Addresses and account numbers for bank accounts and safe deposit boxes you have closed in the past year.
- Information about any unusually large gifts you have made or received.
- Property you have sold in the past year.
- Tax returns and statements of income.
- Statements of expenses.
- Name and balance for your exempt pension plan.
- Mortgage balance.

- Deed or tax bill.

- Car registration.

- Fair market value list for all personal property.

- List of all automatic deductions from your paycheck.

- List of all monthly expenses, including utilities, which are obligations even if they have no ultimate payoff amount.

- All unsecured debt information, including debt on which the creditor does not have any collateral in the item such that it could take the item back from you; for example, unsecured GMAC loans or other loans made to you in which you did not sign a document giving the lender an interest in anything you own, such as your car or boat.

- Information on secured debt such as for cars—account number, monthly payment, and balance owed.

- Car lease paperwork. This is an obligation you made.

- Additional information about your house, such as payoff information.

- Information for any debt for goods and services provided to you, including legal, dental, repairs to your house, vet bills.

- List of anything you owe to anyone that you are not able to pay.


## MEETING WITH A BANKRUPTCY ATTORNEY

If you choose to consult with an attorney, you will feel nervous and fearful at the first meeting. You will also feel stupid and maybe embarrassed unless you are already over that. It is natural. If you are given a questionnaire to complete before you meet with an attorney and you have gathered all of the information as suggested in the preceding lists, at least you will feel on top of it.

If you don't feel prepared, don't worry—the attorney or his or her assistant can walk you through the questionnaire. You can also familiarize yourself with the forms as described in the next chapter. You may not have even half of the information the forms ask for unless you have prepared ahead of time. Help yourself out and arrive at the attorney's office with a bit of preparation and understanding of what you are going to be talking about. These lists should certainly not intimidate you out of prompt filing. It is always good to go into a meeting with an attorney with an agenda other than "Help me, I am drowning." However, don't expect yourself to be perfect. If you need help, ask for it.

## THE PESKY, BUT VITAL INTAKE PROCESS

Different attorneys use different intake processes. *Intake* is the meeting in which the attorney gathers relevant information to assess the case. At the intake, you complete a questionnaire that is used to prepare the actual official bankruptcy filing forms. The official forms are filed with the clerk of the bankruptcy court as original and five copies for Chapters 7 and 13 and the original and six copies for Chapter 11. The bankruptcy clerk for your particular court can provide local rules.

The information you provide about your debts will be applied to a series of schedules for secured, unsecured, and priority debts. If you are still unsure after reading this book, your attorney can assist you in determining the appropriate categories for each of these debts and in determining which are dischargeable in bankruptcy and which are not dischargeable (i.e., the ones you'll be stuck with). Again, if you're still in the dark, the attorney can explain which of your property is exempt (you get to keep it) and which is nonexempt (the trustee may liquidate it to pay your unsecured debtors).

# 7

## Completing the Forms

In this chapter, forms for a voluntary Chapter 7 bankruptcy filing are discussed. We explain each form section to assist you in determining how to complete your own or to help you understand the forms that will be filed on your behalf. At the end of the book, blank forms are provided. However, watch for changes in the law because the forms may change also. Refer to the completed examples of the forms.

## ACKNOWLEDGMENT FORM

The first form you will complete is an acknowledgment that you have read the notice to individual consumer debtors explaining the meaning, purpose, and process of the various bankruptcy chapters. Along with this is the first actual form, Form B1, which indicates that you are filing a Voluntary Petition.

## FORM B1: VOLUNTARY PETITION FORM

The voluntary petition form is a basic information form, which typically includes all of your personal information such as name, address, and telephone number and a box to indicate whether you are an individual, a couple, or a business. You also indicate whether you are filing a Chapter 7 or 13. (We encourage self-filers to attempt only Chapter 7 filings.) The examples here assume, for simplicity purposes, that the filer is an unmarried person filing alone. Couples can file together, but an attorney's advice is probably warranted if a divorce is in the wind or if there are separate assets and debts incurred by each party.

Read page 2 of the voluntary petition form closely to determine where to sign (under perjury). Answer all questions that pertain to you.

## FORM B6: SUMMARY OF SCHEDULES

Although this form comes next in your packet, you should complete this summary of schedules last, after you have completed all of the Schedules A through J that apply to you.

Even though completing the following schedules is going to be tedious, they all must be filed. They may not even remotely apply to you, but they must be filed.

## FORM B6A: SCHEDULE A—REAL PROPERTY

When you file this form, a case number will be assigned to you. This case number must be included on every form amendment, filing, or correspondence. After the *In re* section, include your complete legal name.

On this form, describe any property in which you have an ownership interest. You might feel as if the bank owns your house, but if you are purchasing a house and have any equity, list it here. List the amount owed and the amount of the market value of the property in separate columns.

Remember that *real property* means more than your residence—it includes anything that is real estate. For example, ownership in a time share should be listed. The fine print on these forms explains what to include. However, the language, style, and legalese make it difficult to translate. You may need to read these forms several times to understand what information is being requested.

List each item of real property that you own, that is, house, time share, rental property, small hotel, and unimproved land. Real property is land and the buildings on it; therefore, include condominiums or co-ops as well. The "nature of your interest" means how you own it (see the instructions on the form). Give your best estimate of the current market value of the property. If needed, get an opinion of value from a realtor or perhaps use your tax bill (however, the tax bill is usually under market). Give the full amount of mortgage(s), if any.

## FORM B6B: SCHEDULE B—PERSONAL PROPERTY

This schedule can include many addendum pages because it includes everything you own. It is a "list of all personal property of whatever kind." A couple would indicate property listings as husband's or wife's property.

Before completing this form, refer to our previous advice about "yard sale" value of your personal property. Even though you do not list exempt property here, be aware of which exemption schedule you may elect from federal or your state (if you have the choice). States vary widely in the value of personal property you get to keep.

When completing this form, you may think about what you spent on your items and become disheartened that they would sell for so little at a yard sale or auction. However, in this situation, if the property has less resale value, it is a greater likelihood that you will get to keep it.

## FORM B6C: SCHEDULE C-PROPERTY CLAIMED AS EXEMPT

Refer to the charts accompanying this book to list exempt property. Specify the law providing each exemption (also in the charts). You must state the value of the exemption, (e.g., $5,000 on your homestead real property) and the current market value on the property without deducting the exemption. (Form A accounts for the mortgage.)

As shown in the example filing of a Florida resident, the debtor is entitled to 100 percent of the value of the house as an exemption. This percentage applies in only a few states. The remaining exemptions are modest at best.

## FORM B6D: SCHEDULE D—CREDITORS HOLDING SECURED CLAIMS

This form is self-explanatory.

## FORM B6E: SCHEDULE E—CREDITORS HOLDING UNSECURED PRIORITY CLAIMS

When creditors are unsecured, there is still a pecking order of sorts as to who is paid first. The creditors listed in this schedule have the first bite of the bankruptcy estate apple. It is very important for you to be meticulous in this area because conflict may arise if you omit someone and cannot add him or her later. This form includes a check-list, and you must provide the information for every creditor in this category. This needs careful documentation.

## FORM B6F: SCHEDULE F—CREDITORS HOLDING UNSECURED NONPRIORITY CLAIMS

On this complicated-looking form, list all of your debts, including your specific credit card accounts, account numbers, and amount of balances. If you are organized or have read this book already, you have this neatly tucked in an accordion file according to month and the type of bill.

Follow the form instructions; for each unsecured creditor (not the secured creditors who have threatened to repossess your washer-dryer or your automobile), include all the requested data: last known address, codebtor, if any, and date claim was incurred. For most credit card debt, the answer is "various, miscellaneous consumer debt." If the debt is contingent (i.e., something has to happen before you owe it), indicate with a check in the appropriate box. Also indicate with a check in the appropriate box if debt is disputed (you don't think you owe it).

## FORM B6G: SCHEDULE G-EXECUTORY CONTRACTS AND UNEXPIRED LEASES

As with anything, put on your reading glasses, drink a cup of coffee, and follow the instructions on the form. If you rent, you are the *lessee*.

If you have signed a contract for your boss and the property belongs to him or her, you are the *agent*. In our example, Deborah Debtor did not have anything to include in this schedule.

## FORM B6H: SCHEDULE H—CO-DEBTORS

Again, follow the instructions. A discharge in bankruptcy leaves your cosigner swingin' in the wind (i.e., 100 percent liable for the debt). Our example did not have a codebtor situation.

You are now more than half finished with the process.

## FORM B6I: SCHEDULE I—CURRENT INCOME OF INDIVIDUAL DEBTORS

This schedule requests monthly income; therefore, make necessary adjustments if you are paid weekly or biweekly. Simply refer to your paycheck stubs and list all deductions. Next, list all other income you receive from all sources. Transfer the total to the Summary of Schedules.

## FORM B6J: CURRENT EXPENDITURES OF INDIVIDUAL DEBTORS

On this form, truthfully report your actual expenditures in each category on a monthly basis, annualizing items such as clothing, entertainment (includes holidays), automobile repair, utilities, lawn maintenance (varies by season), car, health, disability and life insurance, and so on. Ignore the items referring to Chapter 12 and 13 filers (They should be doing this with the assistance of an attorney).

## FORM B6J (CONTINUED): DECLARATION CONCERNING DEBTOR'S SCHEDULES

This document is very important to your overall filing. Sign and date the top portion of this form. Supply your name in the top portion of the form that requests "debtor."

## FORM 7: STATEMENT OF FINANCIAL AFFAIRS

The bankruptcy clerk will advise you as to the proper district court to list at the top of this page. Write your complete legal name, and read the instructions and definitions. Next, answer all of the questions. For the majority of the questions, you will probably check the box that says "None." Be sure to sign and date the last page. Do not skip the questions thinking that all are irrelevant—you might find one or two that are relevant. If many of the questions are relevant, this is a clear indication that you should seek legal advice.

## FORM B8: INDIVIDUAL DEBTOR'S STATEMENT OF INTENTION

*This form is very important.* In fact, all of the forms are very important and must be included, even if they don't apply to you. But, Form B8: Debtor's Statement of Intention, is the form for listing your intentions as to secured debts you intend to keep and how you intend to keep them.

If you intend to surrender (give up) an item of secured property, list it on line 2a. For example, your Jaguar XJE, which you absolutely cannot afford to keep making payments on and in which you have a great deal of equity, would be listed here.

On line 2b., list the secured property you intend to keep, such as your house, which you will reaffirm, or continue paying for it. You can also list property you wish to redeem; for example, an above-ground pool. Later, you can cut a deal with the creditor to pay a vastly reduced price to own the pool outright and save the creditor the trouble of coming to take it from your yard. If the Bankruptcy Reform Act is passed, redemption will be of less value—you will have to pay retail value based on the condition of the property.

## VERIFICATION OF CREDITOR MATRIX

The *creditor matrix* form is a complete listing of all of your creditors, including name and address, which is part of your official file. It is also used to contact all of your creditors to inform them of your bankruptcy filing. If an attorney is preparing your petition, he or she will handle all of the finalizing of your documents, including completing the Summary of Schedules with all of the numbers gleaned from the schedules and putting your creditor matrix on a disk for the clerk's office.

## GETTING THE FORMS READY FOR FILING

Now that you have bravely completed the forms, there are a few things you should know about filing them:

- Keep schedules in order when filing.
- Note all the places you have to sign.
- The original (the one you actually signed) must by two-hole punched with five copies or six copies for Chapter 13.

# 8 | What Happens after You File?

If you file your bankruptcy case on your own, you should drop by the bankruptcy clerk's office, tell the clerk that you are doing it yourself, ask for the local rules, and see if he or she has any tips for easy filing. Each bankruptcy office has its own local rules and protocols. They should be glad to help you.

If you do not have all the information needed for your attorney to complete the paperwork, another meeting with your attorney will probably be necessary, unless you can fax the information. Otherwise, the next time you will see your attorney is at the first creditor's meeting. In this meeting, you will be asked all kinds of questions, typically of a very general nature, about what you have listed as assets and other items listed in your filing.

Anyone to whom you owe money will be notified of your bankruptcy filing. It is important that your creditors know what is happening because they have to determine what action to take. Your creditors have options to consider. They have to respond to the notice whether they intend to fight the claim or try to be reaffirmed as debt instead of being completely discharged. In general, your creditors won't object unless they see one or more of the red flags mentioned in previous chapters concerning fraudulent practices, nonpayment history while continuing to charge, cash advances, or luxury purchases within 60 days of filing.

In a Chapter 7 filing, if the trustee determines that there are nonexempt assets to liquidate for distribution to the creditors, the court notifies the creditors and instructs them to file their claims with the court. Priority creditors such as alimony, child support, IRS obligations, attorneys' fees, the trustees' fees, and any other costs of administration of the bankruptcy estate are paid first.

Priority creditors with secured debt may be paid first, and if there is a deficiency after the secured property is liquidated, these creditors may become unsecured priority creditors. For example, if the IRS has a lien against your home and the sale of the home, after satisfaction of all other liens and mortgages, is insufficient to pay the entire lien, the remaining amount becomes an unsecured priority debt. The nonpriority unsecured creditors get a pro rata share of the remaining liquidated nonexempt assets.

In Chapter 13 bankruptcy, creditors can object to the reorganization plan that you are proposing to the court. With the 2002 reform, they may have more ability to object than before, depending on whether the filing was properly prepared under the new rules. There will be more pressure on the individual to pay back the debts that might otherwise have been discharged even within the parameters of repayment. The creditors can also object to the length of time the debtor has to repay the debts.

## VITAL INFORMATION FOR FILING

You want to be prepared to have all of this information included in your filing. But do not be paranoid about it. If you omit something, you will have an opportunity to amend your petition. You may fail to list some assets because you didn't know you had them. For example, you may clean out your basement and find some assets under some dusty old boxes. It's best to add these items as an amendment rather than waiting for the trustee to investigate.

You may simply forget to include some creditors. Many people who are in over their heads have too much happening all at once. It is not unusual for a person to have 10 or more different credit cards. Bills can easily be forgotten, especially if your form of bill triage is to tack them up on your dartboard to determine which one to pay this week. It is a simple matter to amend your petition to include forgotten creditors early on in the process. If you are filing a nonasset Chapter 7, which means none of your unsecured creditors receive anything, it is easy because the creditor cannot complain that he or she was harmed by being forgotten in the first place. If, on the other hand, there was a distribution and the forgotten creditor can complain, he or she probably will, and your amendment may be denied. Do your best to list every creditor the first time. Most attorneys do not want to know about belated amendments without additional fees for the additional work they are required to do.

## BEGINNING THE FILING PROCESS

At the time of filing, you are assigned to a trustee and judge and a meeting of creditors is set. Most of the time, and if you and your attorney get it right, the meeting of creditors is the only time you have to go to the courthouse after you file the papers. The trustee's job is to evaluate your case and process the paperwork, with the primary duty to see that your creditors are paid as much as possible from your nonexempt assets. The trustee is motivated by more than integrity in this process: He or she gets a percentage of any assets recovered for your creditors. If you have done your job right and the trustee has seen nothing to suggest that you have anything up your sleeve, he or she processes your paperwork without investigating your allegations, the creditors get nothing, and you walk away debt free, much wiser, having learned from your past mistakes. This is called a *discharge in bankruptcy.* Having obtained your discharge, you no longer have any legal obligation to pay your creditors, except those with whom you have signed reaffirmation agreements. The court sets a hearing to officially discharge you, thus freeing your nonexempt property from the temporary legal bondage of the trustee. You do not attend this hearing, but the discharge papers are mailed to you. We'll say it again: You should retain all of your bankruptcy papers for life.

People and events you will meet on your path to discharge include:

- *The bankruptcy clerk:* Call the federal courthouse and ask for the office of the bankruptcy clerk. Tell the clerk where you live to make sure you are filing at the right courthouse for your district. When it is time to go to the courthouse to file, take your papers to the bankruptcy clerk. Ask for the local rules and tell the clerk that you are thinking of filing bankruptcy yourself. It is likely that the clerk will be helpful, although he or she cannot give you any legal advice.

- *Attorneys:* As you know, we advise you to hire an attorney you like and feel is competent.

- *Trustee:* The trustee you are assigned is "luck of the draw." To calm your nerves, ask the bankruptcy clerk when he or she is conducting 341 meetings of creditors and sit in for an hour or so. This might desensitize you and help you see how simple it is if you have nothing to hide.

- *341 Creditors' hearing:* The date is assigned the day you file. A notice is mailed to you at the address listed on the petition. You must attend the meeting, or your case will be dismissed.

At the meeting of creditors, secured creditors' representatives appear to ask you about their secured collateral. Be honest. However, don't let them intimidate you into signing anything, no matter how sweet the deal they are offering sounds. The longer you make them wait, the sweeter the deal gets, as a rule.

The 341 creditors' hearing does not always go smoothly. There are many examples of debtors making stupid mistakes that blow their cases wide open and leave them vulnerable to dismissal, whether represented or representing themselves. Keep in mind the old adage: Answer only the question being asked, and keep your answers short and simple. Do not hide anything because you will probably get caught. If you have missed declaring an asset that is nonexempt and the trustee finds out during your hearing, you will look and feel stupid and will be much more highly scrutinized. It is not a good thing to annoy your trustee.

Examples of disasters in the 341 creditors' hearing are legion. Your chances of making some of the more common mistakes increase if you are unrepresented or represented by someone who is inexperienced. However, no one is immune. Lawyers can't always control their clients.

Under questioning by the bankruptcy trustee, the nervous debtor often spills the beans, whether his or her improper asset protection was intentionally fraudulent or innocently undertaken.

The trustee might say: "I notice you don't have a car." The nervous debtor responds: "I had a Cadillac, but I gave it to my brother." Oops! This was an improper transfer for less than fair market value.

Another trustee question might be: "I notice you have a hunting dog worth $25." The debtor responds: "Oh, yes, Old Blue Brummel, my dog, is a grand national champion, won three times in best to show, great stud dog." Uh-oh, undervalued that asset!

Trustees are more suspicious in wealthy areas. A trustee in Palm Beach County, Florida, noticed a woman debtor was obviously clad in expensive designer clothes. Under extensive questioning by the trustee and to her cringing lawyer's chagrin, she confessed that before filing bankruptcy, she had packed up all of her personal property in her home and shipped it to her mother's home out of state. Ouch! Discharge denied. And, she could be prosecuted for perjury, as well (a felony).

Other examples of hearing disasters are:

**Trustee to debtor:** "Gee, a nice Rolex you're wearing. Can I see it?" Proudly, the debtor takes off his watch and hands it over. The trustee takes the watch and puts it to the side.

**Debtor:** "Uh, do I get it back?"

**Trustee:** "You'll have to talk to your attorney about that."

**Trustee:** "Do you have a car?"

**Debtor:** "Yes."

**Trustee:** "How much is it worth?"

**Debtor:** "Oh, about $5,000."

**Trustee:** "Do you have a loan on it?"

**Debtor:** "No."

**Trustee:** "Do you have the keys with you?"

**Debtor:** "Yes."

**Trustee:** "Give them to me and tell me where it's parked."

## PITFALLS YOU CAN AVOID

You can avoid many pitfalls with awareness and careful planning when you are filing yourself or with the help of a paralegal or inexperienced attorney:

- Failing to list all assets.
- Failing to list all debts.
- Failing to assign the property fair market value to your property.

- Overvaluing your property.
- Failure to properly assign exempt property to the exempt category.
- Failure to convert nonexempt property to exempt property pre-bankruptcy in a proper/legal manner.
- Failure to properly complete the documents.
- Failure to respond promptly and properly to requests for additional information from the trustee's office.
- Failure to properly list all of your expenses.
- Failure to properly list your income, sources of income, and deductions.
- Failure to properly use the 60-day rule with cash advances and luxury purchases, including vacations.
- Failure to understand the rule that you have no obligation to enter into reinstatement agreements and/or reaffirmation agreements with creditors and falling victim to creditors seeking to have their debt reinstated after bankruptcy.

With savvy counsel, you may avoid these pitfalls. For example, one client wore her engagement ring with diamonds in it to the hearing; the trustee requested that she take it off her finger, but her attorney objected, noting that the ring was listed in the petition for $100. The disgruntled trustee was left no option but to demand an appraisal supporting the suggested value. This was satisfied by a written statement from a pawnbroker stating that he would buy it for $100.

Don't ever forget that the bankruptcy petitioner is under a strict obligation to tell the truth about assets. Beyond the paper trails that the trustee can pursue, he or she also has the right to physically inspect your house to verify that you have honestly disclosed the personal property you own, although for the average filer, this is an extremely rare occurrence.

## WHAT TO EXPECT

For Chapter 7 filers, the process is a waiting game. You are waiting for it to be over—no transfers of assets until discharge and no credit cards. If any extra money or gifts look imminent, delay the delivery if possible. Delay receiving anything out of the ordinary level of value because everything you have that is not exempt "belongs" to the trustee, and you are under an obligation to inform him or her of any significant changes to your financial situation.

If you are living with a Chapter 13 bankruptcy, it is a little tougher because it won't feel as if it is over. You are going to be living with the plan for whatever period has been agreed on—at least three years. In most situations, your paycheck will be garnished so your employer will send money to the trustee, and a strict budget will be enforced. If you have an unexpected problem such as a leaky roof and you pay for it, then you don't have money to pay into the plan, you must modify your plan. If your income goes down and you cannot pay according to your agreement, your bankruptcy will be dismissed, and you will lose your assets. Your only option at that juncture would be to file for Chapter 7 bankruptcy.

If you have filed Chapter 7, you will have your meeting with creditors. After the meeting of creditors, there is a mandatory 60-day waiting period during which creditors must file their objections or claims if the trustee determines that there are nonexempt assets to liquidate and distribute to the creditors.

Assuming yours is a no-asset case (you have only exempt assets or assets the trustee isn't interested in), you should receive your *discharge in bankruptcy* in the mail. This is your proof that you no longer owe the debts in the bankruptcy other than the ones you reaffirmed. Congratulations! You have received your *fresh start!* Use it well.

# 9 | Life after Bankruptcy and How to Cultivate Your Credit

Now that you understand credit, begin getting on your feet by destroying any of the offers that come in the mail saying you are preapproved. When credit card companies solicit your business by phone, tell them no! Just hang up if you have to. If you are at the airport and see a table where a company is offering you a gift if you sign up for its low-interest credit card, run. There are all kinds of insidious ways credit card companies entice you. Be strong! Resist temptation.

## AVOID THE QUICK FIX

Chances are that looking for a quick fix is at least part of what created your bankruptcy. Resist the urge to fall for a quick fix to repair the damage. Typical claims include:

We can erase your bad credit.
Legally create a new credit identity.
We can wipe bankruptcies and judgments off your slate forever.

The reality is that only time, effort, and a debt repayment plan can improve your credit report and rating. There are legitimate organizations that do this type of work, but check them out through the Better Business Bureau to be sure they are operating according to legal standards.

## RED FLAGS

Steer clear if a company does any of the following:

- Asks for payment before any services are rendered. (Under the Credit Repair Organizations Act, credit repair companies cannot require you to pay until they have completed the promised services.)
- Recommends that you dispute the information on your credit report.
- Suggests that you take any action that seems to be illegal, such as creating a new credit identity. Committing fraud makes you liable for prosecution. (It's a federal crime to falsify statements on a loan or credit application or to purposely misrepresent your social security number. It is also a federal offense to obtain an Employer ID number from the IRS under false pretenses.)
- Does not explain your legal rights.
- Does not inform you of what you can do yourself.
- Tells you *not* to contact a credit bureau directly.

## THE BOTTOM LINE

Regardless of the claims some companies make, no one can legally remove information from a credit report if that information is accurate and timely. However, you are permitted by law to ask for a reinvestigation of information on your report that you believe is inaccurate or not complete. You can obtain your credit report at no charge, and you can clear and rebuild your own credit without the assistance of an outside agency.

According to the Fair Credit Reporting Act:

- You are entitled to a free copy of your credit report if you've been denied credit, insurance, or employment within the last 60 days. If your application for credit, insurance, or employment is denied because of information supplied by a credit bureau, the company you applied to must provide you with that credit bureau's name, address, and telephone number.

- You can dispute mistakes or outdated items without cost. Request a dispute form from the credit-reporting agency or send them a written letter with all pertinent information. (Send photocopies and keep the originals.)

### How to Dispute Inaccurate Information

- Identify each item that you dispute.

- Explain the specific reasons for disputing each item and request a reinvestigation.

- If the new investigation reveals a mistake, ask that a corrected version of the report be sent to everyone who received your credit report within the past six months.

    The credit bureau is required to give you the written results of the reinvestigation when it is completed. If the reinvestigation resulted in a change on your credit report, the bureau must give you an updated free copy. (See more on this in the next section.)

- If the reinvestigation does not resolve your dispute, instruct the credit bureau to include your version of the dispute in your file and in future reports.

## HOW LONG WILL "NEGATIVE INFORMATION" HAUNT YOU?

In most cases, accurate negative information can remain on your report for seven years. The following are exceptions:

- Bankruptcy information can be reported for 10 years.

- Information reported because of a job application for a position with a salary of more than $75,000 has no time limitation.

- Information reported because of an application for more than $150,000 worth of credit or life insurance has no time limitation.

## BUILT-IN PROTECTIONS

Credit repair organizations are required to provide you with a copy of the "Consumer Credit File Rights Under State and Federal Law" before you sign a contract. The contract must specify your rights and obligations. Read everything *twice* before you sign it.

For your legal protection, a credit repair company cannot:

- Charge you until it has completed the promised services.
- Falsify claims about its services.
- Perform any services until you have signed a written contract and have completed a three-day waiting period. (You have 72 hours after signing the contract to cancel it without paying any fees.)

Your contract must:

- Specify the terms of payment including the total cost.
- Give a detailed description of the services to be performed.
- Indicate how long it will take to achieve the results.
- Detail any guarantees offered.
- Include the company's name, business address, and phone number.

## GET THE LEGITIMATE HELP YOU NEED

If you feel that you cannot handle resolving your credit problems by yourself, consider contacting a credit counseling service. Nonprofit organizations are in existence in every state to assist and counsel consumers in debt. These organizations arrange payment plans that are acceptable to you and your creditors. They also can help you create a realistic budget. Find the office closest to you by checking the Yellow Pages of your telephone directory.

## REBUILD YOUR CREDIT WITH A SECURED CARD

You can obtain a secured credit card from your bank. You are actually "borrowing against" your own money that is placed in a savings account at the bank. The funds in your savings account "secure" your potential debt. You cannot withdraw from this account until you close the card account or the bank desecures it. If you default on your card debt, the bank will take funds from your savings account to pay the bill.

## YOUR CREDIT REPORT

Your credit report—a type of consumer report—contains information about where you work and live and how you pay your bills. It also may show whether you've been sued or arrested or have filed for bankruptcy. Companies called consumer reporting agencies (CRAs) or credit bureaus compile and sell your credit report to businesses. Because businesses use this information to evaluate your applications for credit, insurance, employment, and other purposes allowed by the Fair Credit Reporting Act (FCRA), it's important that the information in your report be complete and accurate.

Some financial advisors suggest that you periodically review your credit report for inaccuracies or omissions. This could be especially important if you're considering making a major purchase, such as buying a home. Checking in advance on the accuracy of information in your credit file could speed the credit-granting process.

## GETTING YOUR CREDIT REPORT

If you've been turned down for a credit card, loan, insurance policy, or employment because of information supplied by a CRA, the FCRA says the company you applied to must give you the CRA's name, address, and telephone number. Contact the agency for a copy of your report within 60 days of receiving a denial notice and the report is free. You're also entitled to a free copy of your report if you certify in writing that you're unemployed and plan to look for a job within 60 days, you're on welfare, or your credit report is inaccurate because of fraudulent activity. Otherwise, it may cost up to $9 for a copy of your report.

If you simply want a copy of your report, call the CRAs listed in the Yellow Pages under "credit" or "credit rating and reporting." Call each credit bureau listed because more than one agency may have a file on you, some with different information.

The three major national credit bureaus are:

1. Equifax, P.O. Box 740241, Atlanta, GA 30374–0241; (800) 685–1111.
2. Experian (formerly TRW), P.O. Box 2002, Allen, TX 75013; (888) EXPERIAN or (888) 397–3742.
3. Trans Union, P.O. Box 1000, Chester, PA 19022; (800) 916–8800.

## CORRECTING ERRORS

Under the FCRA, both the consumer reporting agency (CRA)and the organization that provided the information to the CRA, such as a bank or credit card company, have responsibilities for correcting inaccurate or incomplete information in your report. To protect all your rights under the law, contact both the CRA and the information provider.

First, tell the CRA in writing what information you believe is inaccurate. Include copies (*not* originals) of documents that support your position. In addition to providing your complete name and address, your letter should clearly identify each item in your report that you dispute, state the facts and explain why you are disputing the information, and request deletion or correction. You may want to enclose a copy of your report with the items in question circled. Your letter may look something like the sample that follows. Send your letter by certified mail, return receipt requested, to document what the CRA received. Keep copies of your dispute letter and enclosures.

CRAs must reinvestigate the items in question—usually within 30 days—unless they consider your dispute frivolous. They also must forward all relevant data you provide about the dispute to the information provider. After the information provider receives notice of a dispute from the CRA, it must investigate, review all relevant information provided by the CRA, and report the results to the CRA. If the information provider finds the disputed information to be inaccurate, it must notify all nationwide CRAs so they can correct this information in your file. Disputed information that cannot be verified must be deleted from your file.

If your report contains erroneous information, the CRA must correct it. If an item is incomplete, the CRA must complete it. For example, if your file showed that you were late making payments, but failed to show that you were no longer delinquent, the CRA must show that you're current.

If your file shows an account that belongs to another person, the CRA must delete it. When the reinvestigation is complete, the CRA must give you the written results and a free copy of your report if the dispute results in a change. If an item is changed or removed, the CRA cannot put the disputed information back in your file unless the information provider verifies its accuracy and completeness, and the CRA gives you a written notice that includes the name, address, and phone number of the provider.

Also, if you request, the CRA must send notices of corrections to anyone who received your report in the past six months. Job applicants can have a corrected copy of their report sent to anyone who received a copy during the past two years for employment purposes. If a reinvestigation does not resolve your dispute, ask the CRA to include your statement of the dispute in your file and in future reports.

In addition to writing to the CRA, tell the creditor or other information provider in writing that you dispute an item. Again, include copies (*not* originals) of documents that support your position. Many providers specify an address for disputes. If the provider then reports the item to any CRA, it must include a notice of your dispute. In addition, if you are correct—that is, if the disputed information is not accurate—the information provider may not use it again.

When negative information in your report is accurate, only the passage of time can ensure its removal. Accurate negative information can generally stay on your report for seven years. There are certain exceptions, including:

- Information about criminal convictions may be reported without any time limitation.
- Bankruptcy information may be reported for 10 years.

  Remember:

- Credit information reported in response to an application for a job with a salary of more than $75,000 has no time limit.
- Credit information reported because of an application for more than $150,000 worth of credit or life insurance has no time limit.
- Information about a lawsuit or an unpaid judgment against you can be reported for seven years or until the statute of limitations runs out, whichever is longer.

## *Adding Accounts to Your File*

Your credit file may not reflect all your credit accounts. Although most national department store and all-purpose bank credit card accounts are included in your file, not all creditors supply information to CRAs: Some travel, entertainment, gasoline card companies, local retailers, and credit unions are among those creditors that don't. If you've been told you were denied credit because of an "insufficient credit file" or "no credit file" and you have accounts with creditors that don't appear in your credit file, ask the CRA to add this information to future reports. Although they are not required to do so, many CRAs will add verifiable accounts for a fee. You should, however, understand that if these creditors do not report to the CRA on a regular basis, these added items will not be updated in your file.

## MODIFYING YOUR LIFESTYLE

As you have learned, in a Chapter 7 bankruptcy you can be fully discharged from most of your debts, but you may have to lose many of your assets. You may find that you have much less than you had in the way of luxury items. If you were able to transform much of your nonexempt property to cash before you filed your bankruptcy, you are probably left with a much simpler lifestyle. You are probably pretty bare bones compared to what you had before you filed.

This can be very freeing, but it can also be a shock to you after the dust of discharge settles. You have many decisions to make. You have choices about how you now want to live your life. There is nothing wrong with wanting to rebuild your life so that you obtain the things and the lifestyle you once had. However, be very circumspect as you design what this new life is going to look like to you and how you are going to go about building it.

Many people find that the worst part about Chapter 7 bankruptcy is that they lose their ability to obtain credit cards and other forms of credit. You will be surprised how many people know about your discharge and who will solicit your business to sign up for credit cards and loans. You might even feel special and important as you receive letters saying, "We are so sorry you fell onto hard times, but we are here to help you get on your feet."

Credit card companies and loan companies want your business because they know you now have little or no unsecured debt. You are a newborn babe who is so desperate to rejoin the spending world that you are willing to regain credit no matter what it costs you. Do not be tempted.

Credit offers post-bankruptcy have such exorbitant interest rates that they should be accused of usury. It is blood money, demons knocking at your door. Resist. Take your time and think about how you are going to rebuild. Strategy is your best friend.

Post-Chapter 7 bankruptcy, you will, at least theoretically, have what you need to get a fresh start. Although this means different things in different states, you should be able to afford the basics. And if you are not disabled, you should be able to begin the rebuilding of your assets. You are not precluded from earning money simply because you filed for bankruptcy. The purpose of the filing is to find a way to handle the debts incurred before the bankruptcy case is opened. You are not haunted by the creditors of Christmases past.

One of the things you might want to get used to post-bankruptcy is using cash for purchases. It is very enlightening to spend exactly what you earn without relying on the stretching ability of a credit card. If you want to buy something or your children want to buy something, do it the old-fashioned way: Save up for it. Think about the days before the Diner's Card changed the course of history by creating the first form of plastic credit. What did people do if they wanted something? Many people "bought on time," which is the same thing as credit. Layaway is a good possibility because it does not involve interest payments and you can pay a little at a time toward something you need or want. You will think about what you are spending and get into the habit of planning.

If you have steady income, you merely need to change your consciousness about money. You don't want to find yourself back in the situation you were in before you filed. No one wants to purposely bring that kind of pressure on himself or herself.

Make a list of your monthly expenses that are set into stone. See if you can afford them. If you are stuck with a mortgage that you reaffirmed in your Chapter 7 bankruptcy, see if it still keeps you too stretched financially to make it worthwhile to hold onto it. If you are still sweating it, move. It is very difficult to give up things you think you need. A house represents more than anything else we own. How can you feel comfortable in a house that you know you can't afford?

You are not fully finished with your bankruptcy discharge until you clean up all the loose ends after the legal process is complete. You might still owe back taxes. You know that they are not dischargeable. You must factor them into the equation. There are many ways to approach the IRS, such as what is called an "Offer in Compromise"; however, you should certainly discuss any tax matters of any consequence with a lawyer. The IRS is often tricky and the specific details of approaching them post-bankruptcy are beyond the scope of this book. As you consider how to rebuild your life, you need to factor in payments for some of your nondischargeable debts. Particularly with the bankruptcy reform, you may find that certain debts that might have been discharged are not, for example, back taxes.

So, look at your overall picture before you decide what kind of lifestyle you want. Think about what a fresh start means to you. You might want to sit down as a family or as a couple and think about what your goals are. Make sure they are in agreement. If one of you wants simplicity and the other wants to fight to rebuild a high standard of living, you have to either compromise or duke it out.

Whatever you decide to do, you need to take it slowly. After discharge, if you need to replace a car that was repossessed or lost during the process, you might want to purchase a car even if you pay a higher interest rate. Buying a modest car without the bells and whistles is one of the best ways to begin to show credit worthiness. Do not do this unless you know that you have an income stream that will support on-time payments. What people do not realize is that paying on time is sometimes more important in the overall evaluation of you as a credit risk than whether you have had a bankruptcy. What you do now is in your hands.

Pay your bills on time. In general, do not become lax. This is why you should look at what obligations are left after discharge. Don't look at your circumstances as "What can I cling to?" Look at them as "What can I unload so I can reduce my obligations as much as possible?" Things are not important in the scheme of your life. You can replace most things and, unless they are sentimental, most are more of a burden than a benefit.

Pare down and rebuild slowly. Think of it as having ended a relationship. What you do during the rebound period is important. It is when you are most vulnerable.

If you really must, send for one, maybe two, credit cards. Again, it is more important to show how steady your payments are in establishing a picture of who you are today. Try not to max out the card and pay the balance in full at the end of the month. It is good to use the card to show that you can pay the bill off easily, but do not create the appearance of falling right back into your old ways.

## FOLLOWING BANKRUPTCY

After a bankruptcy, the details of the procedure are listed in your credit report. There are those three main credit bureaus available as resources for potential creditors. Any time you apply for credit, you will be evaluated by the information found in the report of one or all of the reports they provide. Most people typically do not consider building strong credit before problems arise. Credit is easy to come by but not always easy to maintain. If you are not careful, before you know it you are having problems, and you have so-called *black marks* on a report that you typically will never see. Creditors make decisions on your life by looking at information about you that may not even be correct. The system is not infallible. Unless you find out what is on the report, it is like gossip behind your back. You will never know why you are rejected.

## THINGS MAY NOT BE AS BAD AS YOU THINK

After a bankruptcy, however, you can pretty well figure out why you might be turned down for credit. The problem is that you may assume things are worse than they are. After a period of time beyond the date of discharge, you appear as less of a credit risk and it is reflected on your credit score.

This is why it is important for you to look at your credit report and make efforts to clean it up as best as possible. Dispute any incorrect information or supply explanations as to why problems arose with certain payments.

To obtain a copy of your credit report, you must provide the following in writing:

- Full name, including any previous names.
- Current address.
- Previous address (if needed for five-year credit history).
- Social security number.
- Date of birth.
- Signature.

Follow through with your cleanup and you will be more in control than you could imagine. You can do it right this time and continue your financial life on strong footing.

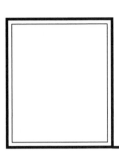

# Epilogue—Bankruptcy Reform and How It Will Affect the World as We Know It

The bankruptcy reform that is looming over the horizon is not new. Many versions have been proposed. The current reform continues to be tabled for many reasons, but most practitioners believe it is simply a matter of time. Therefore, we have included this epilogue and have referred to the implications of the reform throughout the book so you will be prepared.

Bankruptcies are at an all-time high. Some statistics reveal that business bankruptcies in 2002 reached epic proportions not seen since the period immediately following World War II. The year 2002 was a continuation of a trend that was begun years before, particularly in the 1990s when businesses invested in companies that were underfunded.

Business filings of major corporate giants who are seeking Chapter 11 protection trickle down into the lives of consumers.

Your financial crises influence the health of the retailers. It is to everyone's advantage to straighten out the economy with each of us making the effort to change that small piece of it that we can control: our own finances, our consciousness about credit and spending, and the opportunities a fresh start affords us.

## STATISTICS ARE STAGGERING

In the first three quarters of 2002, over 1,181,004 bankruptcies were filed. Of those filings, 1,152,103 were personal bankruptcies, both

Chapter 7 and Chapter 13. These are the most current statistics available through the American Bankruptcy Institute.

It is evident that the economy has changed the way we have to conduct our financial lives. As we have indicated in this book, it is best, if at all possible, for you to avoid having to file bankruptcy. If you do file, there will be implications for you when the new reform is passed that will make it more difficult for you to have the same relief you would have had prior to its passage.

This epilogue explains the many implications the reform will have for those who seek bankruptcy protection. One of the main changes is that the reform will strictly regulate who can qualify for Chapter 7 relief. That is, it will provide guidelines specifying whether or not you have the ability to repay your unsecured credit card balances and other unsecured debt. The proposed changes regarding your income and qualifications are called *means testing*, and involve three key elements:

1. The definition of your monthly income,
2. The list of allowed deductions, and
3. Specific income *trigger points* (as the reformers call them) that determine whether you will be allowed to file a Chapter 7 petition.

Here is how the reforms will work:

- If the new Federal Bankruptcy Law passes, your "current" monthly income will not be your actual current income, but an average of your monthly income over the six months preceding the determination, including any contributions others that live with you may make to the household. This is a far cry from the standards applied under the current law, which take into consideration only your own actual monthly income at the time of filing.

- The list of deductions under the new law are based on the standards as set by the IRS, and not your actual expenses. The *trigger points* define whether or not you can file for Chapter 7 relief. If you have $166.67 remaining after all allowed deductions from your average monthly income, you don't qualify, regardless of the magnitude of your unsecured debt. If you have $100.00 per month left over, and that is enough to pay at least 25 percent of your unsecured debt over five years, you will be required to file under Chapter 13.

The process of bankruptcy is not a panacea. The new bankruptcy reform legislation will not give easy full debt relief as in the past. Under the new laws, many more people will be forced to file a Chapter 13 and submit a repayment plan that obligates them to repay a portion of their debt to their creditors over time. In states with generous exemption schemes, many of these exemptions will be limited by the new reform legislation. Rather than allowing deductions for your actual expenditures for your basic requirements of living such as housing, transportation, utilities, food, clothing, and entertainment, the standard deduction as set by the IRS for your region of the country will be applied. Among other things, this means debtors will have to give up more property to their creditors and will have less leeway with regard to luxury purchases and cash advances.

While the reform is the result of lobbying by the credit card industry to make it much more difficult for debtors to discharge their debts in bankruptcy, the result will mean that truly insolvent debtors will be unable to find relief. The intent of the reform is to weed out those who can, over time, get themselves out of debt. We have included information about debt counseling and ways to avoid having to file, because we need to make a change in the way we look at spending and debt accumulation. Although the credit card companies dangle the carrot of easy money and "get-it-now" spending, we, as consumers, need to resist. Credit card companies want to cut their losses. We, as consumers, want to avoid falling into the never-ending black hole of exorbitant interest payments.

The reform will make changes. However, the bankruptcy laws will remain concrete and tangible. If you are facing potential bankruptcy, advance planning is always your best option. Protect your assets as best you can and make sure to consult professionals about both credit counseling and the bankruptcy laws.

Chapter 13 will also be changed by the bankruptcy reform. The filing will be more difficult due to changes in the standards under which you qualify. It will also be more difficult to work out the Chapter 13 reorganization plan for repayment of creditors while discharging certain qualified debts. The difficulty of the filing will depend largely on the procedures in place in the state where you reside.

For example, in the Southern District of Florida, many changes to Chapter 13 under the new laws are already in place. These include:

- Mandatory wage deduction orders requiring employers to withhold plan payments from your paycheck and send them to the Chapter 13 Trustee.

- Must be current on filings with IRS or have to incorporate maximum annual assessments into plan payment (could be as high as $25,000.00/year).

- Close scrutiny of finances of Chapter 13 debtors who are small business owners.

- Disallows voluntary contributions into pension or retirement plans or savings plans during the Chapter 13 plan. Certain other payments may be disallowed, such as payments for timeshare units.

Because bankruptcy is not to be taken lightly in any event, and because of the pending changes in the law, we have included a chapter on how credit works and how you might be able to dig your way out without seeking bankruptcy protection. Part of the reform will be to require that you have made best efforts to rearrange your debt before you can be considered for bankruptcy protection.

## SYNOPSIS OF THE PENDING LEGISLATION

Here is a more detailed synopsis of the Pending Bankruptcy Abuse Prevention and Consumer Act taken from the Joint Explanatory Statement of the Committee of the Conference as found online at Commercial Law League of America:

*The proposed changes in the law set forth herein are the result of a Committee meeting wherein the House and Senate worked out the differences in their two bills. Unless we learn differently, this probably is how the legislation will pass.*

- Rather than the current standard of a presumption in favor of granting the debtor a discharge absent a showing of a substantial abuse of the provisions of the code, under the new code, a presumption of abuse would be found where the debtor's income minus the allowable deductions exceeds 25 percent of his out-standing nonpriority unsecured debt, or $6,000.00, (whichever is greater), or $10,000. The allowable deductions include those basic living expenses as determined by the IRS for your region, certain other expenses in their actual amount determined acceptable "other necessary" expenses by the IRS, and reasonably necessary expenses for maintain safety of debtor and family, the debtors average monthly payments on account of secured debts and priority claims, and if the debtor is under Chapter 13, the actual administrative expenses for the district in which a debtor resides, up to 10 percent of the plan payments (pp. 1–3, formula at page 3 for payments on secured debts, priority claims).

- Requires filing new form for current income showing that no presumption of abuse applies showing calculations that determine if a presumption of abuse applies and how each amount is calculated. The presumption may be rebutted by the debtor under very restricted circumstances (p. 5).

- The court or interested party can still bring a motion to dismiss for bad faith filing in which the debtor and /or his attorney may be held liable for costs and possible penalties against the debtor's attorney if found to violate rule 9011 (p. 6).

- Safe Harbors with respect to above: No motion to dismiss if the debtor's income falls below the state median family income for an individual or a family of its size (p. 7).

- Income redefined to include all income taxable and nontaxable averaged over the last six-month period prior to filing. It includes contributions made on a regular basis to the debtor for household expenses for his expenses and those of his children, by others, including the wife. Excludes Social Security payments, and payments to victims of war crimes or acts of terrorism.

- Requires report by Trustee to court as to whether or not based on their review, the filing is a abuse. If court concurs that it is, notice is given to creditors and Trustee must file a motion to dismiss within 30 days. Notice is given to creditors.

- Case can be dismissed if bankruptcy discharge would hurt victim of crime of violence or drug trafficking. Where debtor is perpetrator and can't show genuine need to file based on domestic support obligations.

- Requires good faith finding in Chapter 13 cases (p. 10).

- Requires notice to consumer debtors of alternatives to bankruptcy filing, and establishes a pilot program of credit counseling services.

- Requires an individual as a condition of eligibility for relief to receive credit counseling within the 180-day period preceding filing.

- The debtor is also required to complete a financial management course.

## In Title II Enhanced Consumer Protections

- *Subtitle A:* Debtor may reduce the balance owed by 20 percent if he can show that greater than 60 before filing Creditor refused good faith payment plan under which creditor would have received 60 percent of balance owed (p. 16). Other abuses by creditors addressed here, overhauling reaffirmation agreements, failure to properly attribute payments to the balance owed.

- *Subtitle B—Priority child support:* Support alimony and maintenance payments are priority whether court ordered or not.

- *Abusive practices by creditors* with regard to reaffirmation agreements and failure to properly credit payments made under a confirmed Chapter 11, 12, or 13 plan are penalized.

- *Automatic deductions by your employer* representing payments against loans to your qualified pension plan will be allowed, and such amounts will not be considered part of your disposable income, and such loans are not dischargeable in either Chapter 7 or 13 filings.

- *One million dollar cap* on the exempt value of an individual debtor's interest in an individual retirement account that a debtor may claim as exempt property (p. 28).

- *Protection of education savings in bankruptcy:* Funds, not to exceed $5,000.00, placed in an educational retirement account not later than 365 days before filing are exempt providing the designated beneficiary of such account is a child, stepchild, grandchild, or step-grandchild of the debtor for the taxable year during which funds were placed in the account. May possibly include foster child or adopted child (p. 26).

*Title III Discouraging Bankruptcy Abuse (p. 34)*

- *Reinforcement of the fresh start.*

- *Discourages bad faith repeat filings:* Terminates automatic stay within 30 days in a Chapter 7, 11, or 13 case filed by or against an individual if such party was a debtor in a previously dismissed case pending within the preceding one-year period.

- *Adds a new ground for relief from the automatic stay* where claim is secured by an interest in real property and court finds that the filing of the case was part of a scheme to delay, hinder, or defraud certain creditors in regard to the transfer of an ownership interest without consent of creditor, or multiple filings affecting the real property.

- *Requires debtor to reaffirm or redeem secured personal property* within 45 days after the first meeting of creditors, if not, property is no longer subject to automatic stay, likewise with regard to the property referred to in the debtor's statement of intention if debtor fails to take action as stated in his statement of intention (38, p. 37).

- *Residency—Domiciliary requirements for exemptions:* Debtor must be domiciled (statement of intention to reside in the subject state, may require filing certain documents and proof of actual residence) in a state 730 days (as opposed to the current 180 days) before he may claim that state's exemptions. If debtor's domicile has not been located in a single state for the 730-day period, then the state where the debtor was domiciled for the 180-day period preceding the 730-day period controls. If the effect of this provision is to render the debtor ineligible for any state exemption, then the federal exemption controls, notwithstanding any states opt out.

- *Reduction of homestead exemption for fraud* (p. 40). Reduces the value of the debtor's interest in the following property that may be claimed as exempt under certain circumstances:

  —Real or personal property that the debtor or a dependent of the debtor uses as a residence (including condos, mobile homes, cooperatives) burial plot, real or personal property that the debtor or dependent of debtor claims as a homestead. Where nonexempt property is converted to the above specified exempt property within the 10-year period preceding the filing of the bankruptcy case, the exemption must be reduced to the extent that such value was acquired with the intent to hinder, delay, or defraud a creditor (p. 40).

- *Limitations on luxury goods:* Luxury goods or services incurred within 90 days of filing in an aggregate amount of $500.00 are presumed to be nondischargeable. Cash advances aggregating more than $750.00 that are incurred within 70 days are nondischargeable. The term *luxury goods and services* does not include those necessary for the support or maintenance of debtor or her dependents (p. 42).

- *Automatic stay* (p. 43): The conference report excepts from the automatic stay a judgment of eviction with respect to a residential household under the most common circumstances. That is, if a debtor is in the process of being evicted for nonpayment or for illegal activity, the stay has no effect and the eviction proceeding can go forward without delay.

- *Extension of period between bankruptcy filings:* A Chapter 7 debtor may only file another Chapter 7 after a period of eight years (up from the current 6 year period. A Chapter 13 filing may only follow a Chapter 7 filing by four years. A Chapter 13 filing may follow a previous Chapter 13 filing by two years.

- *Certain as yet unspecified restrictions* are placed on the definition of what constitutes "household goods," but excepting from that definition electronic equipment, antiques and jewelry above a certain monetary threshold, and specifies that works of art are not household goods, unless created by the debtor or any relative of the debtor.

- *Evidence of income and tax returns* (p. 48): The debtor is must file:

  1. Copies of all evidence of payments by employers within 60 days preceding filing.

  2. An itemized statement of the amount of monthly net income, itemized to show how such amount is calculated.

  3. A statement disclosing any anticipated increase in income or expenditures in the 12-month period following the date of filing.

In addition,

  4. The debtor is required to provide a copy of his or her federal income tax return for the latest taxable period ending prior to

the filing, or the case will be dismissed. During the pendency of a Chapter 7, 11, or 13 case upon the request of any party in interest (trustee, judge, creditor) the debtor must provide tax returns and all amendments that were not filed for the three-year period preceding the date on which the order for relief was entered.

- Chapter 13 debtors must:

  1. File a statement of income and expenditures in the preceding tax year and monthly income showing how the amounts were calculated, annually.

  2. The statement must disclose all sources of income and amounts.

  3. Identify all contributors to support of debtor and her dependents.

  4. Identify any persons who contribute(d) to debtor's household expenses, and amounts.

  The new reform eliminates the current law enabling a debtor to discharge tax debts in certain circumstances. The Reform will prohibit the discharge of those certain tax claims as well as claims for a tax required to be collected or withheld and for which the debtor is liable in whatever capacity. (It seems as though we must say goodbye to miracle Chapter 13 relief for old IRS tax liens.)

- *Limitations on homestead exemptions:* The new section 322(a) amends the code to impose an aggregate monetary limitation of $125,000.00 on the value of property that the debtor may claim as exempt under state or local law under certain circumstances. The monetary cap applies if the debtor acquired the property within the 1215-day period preceding the filing of the petition and the property consists of any real or personal property that the debtor or dependant of the debtor claims as a homestead. This limit doesn't apply to a family farmer, nor does it apply to any interest transferred from a debtor's principal residence which was acquired prior to the beginning of the specified time period to the debtor's current principal residence, if both the previous an current residences are located in the same state.

- *Section 322 further amends the section 522* to add a provision that does not allow a debtor to exempt any amount of an interest in property in excess of 125,000 if any of the following applies (p. 54).

- *A debtor convicted of a felony* which under the circumstances the filing of the case was an abuse of the bankruptcy code.

- *The debtor owes a debt arising from:* violation of federal securities laws; fraud, deceit, or manipulation in a fiduciary capacity in connection with the sale, or purchase of any registered security; any civil remedy under section 1964 of title 18 of the U.S. Code; any criminal act, intentional tort, or willful or reckless misconduct that caused serious injury or death in the preceding 5 years.

- *An exception to the monetary limit* may be shown to be reasonably necessary for the support of the debtor and any dependent of the debtor.

- *The taxing authority may request a dismissal* of a pending action where a debtor fails to file a postpetition tax return or obtain an extension.

- *The new provisions require that the Chapter 13 debtor be current* on the last four years of filing required IRS tax returns. Currently, a debtor can enjoy the benefits of filing even though delinquent in the filing of tax returns. Under the new rules, the delinquent Chapter 13 debtor faces dismissal or conversion to a Chapter 7 after notice and a hearing. This means the potential sale of nonexempt assets to pay off the debts while the debtor had wanted to avoid complete liquidation.

## DON'T BE INTIMIDATED BY THE LANGUAGE AND IMPLICATIONS OF THE REFORM

While it will make certain aspects of bankruptcy more difficult, it does not eliminate all of the advantages if you find yourself in an untenable position. If you have exhausted your possibilities in changing your status, this is what you need to do to rebuild your future. If you file after the passage of the reform, whenever, and some say, if ever it passes, be sure to seek advice from an attorney who has knowledge of the law. Then you will be on the road to full financial recovery.

# APPENDIXES

**Automatic stay:**   While your bankruptcy case is pending, you have what is called an *automatic stay*, which immediately upon receiving notice of the filing of your petition, stops your creditors from being able to collect from you, with certain exceptions and conditions.

**Bankruptcy:**   A procedure that is governed by Title 11 of the United States Code, administered through the federal courts. Filing for bankruptcy relief means submitting a petition to the federal courts asking the court to consider your entire financial situation and give you relief from your debts.

**Blue book value:**   A term used for information (obtainable on the Web) that lists the fair market value of personal property, most commonly used to price your vehicle.

**Chapter 7 bankruptcy:**   A chapter of the U.S. Bankruptcy Code that provides for a complete discharge of many debts, for individuals, married couples filing jointly, and business entities.

**Chapter 13 bankruptcy:**   A chapter of the U.S. Bankruptcy Code that provides a debtor to create a payment plan to pay off some or all of his creditors over 36 or 60 months.

**Chapter 13 repayment plan:**   A plan filed with the bankruptcy court setting forth how much you are going to pay your creditors over either a three-year, or five-year period of time. The amount of the repayment is based on an estimate of your future income.

**Codebtor:**   An individual who is jointly obligated to repay a debt. Often known as the cosigner.

**Contingent debt:**   A debt that will only come into being on the occurrence of some future event.

**Credit counseling service:**   An organization that will look at your total financial picture and attempt to negotiate with you creditors to accept a reasonable payoff, either as a lump sum payment, if you can swing it, or a repayment plan you can live with.

**Creditor:**   A person or entity that is owed a debt.

**Debt:**   Money you owe to the creditor (the one who extended goods and services to you based on your written or oral promise to pay). Debt is usually of two basic types: secured and unsecured.

**Deficiency judgment:**   Often, if the secured property is no longer of sufficient value to cover the debt, you will be personally sued for the deficiency. In bankruptcy you can discharge the deficiency, but the property itself will go to the creditor, unless you redeem it, or reaffirm the debt.

**Discharge:**   A legal excuse of why you no longer have to pay your debts, basically wiping out your debt (called a Chapter 7 discharge in bankruptcy) or force your unsecured creditors to accept a payment plan wherein they will receive only a portion of what you actually owe them, and with regard to the unpaid balance you receive a discharge (in a Chapter 13 bankruptcy). Discharge also refers to your release from the bankruptcy court at the end of the bankruptcy case.

**Dischargeable debt:**   The kind of debt that bankruptcy laws allow you to wipe out in bankruptcy. Unsecured credit cards balances, unsecured loans from loan companies, department store credit cards, and medical bills are good examples. So are personal loans from friends and family. These are called consumer debts and are the kind of debt that lands most of debtors in the bankruptcy courts.

**Disputed debt:**   A debt that you believe you do not owe, or on which there is no agreement as to the amount owed.

**Equity:**   The difference between what your property is currently worth, that is, what it would sell for in the market today, often referred to as its "fair market value," and what your owe on it, if anything. For example, if houses like yours in your neighborhood are currently selling for $150,000.00 and your mortgage balance is $75,000.00, your equity in your home is $75,000.00. Likewise, if your automobile would bring $10,000.00 if you put it in the local "car trader" and sold it, and the outstanding balance on your auto loan is $8,000.00, then your equity is $2,000.00

**Executory contract:**   An incomplete contract, in which one or both of the parties have failed to satisfy their obligations.

**Exemptions:**   Certain assets are exempt from collection efforts by creditors and by the bankruptcy courts. Exempt property is property that cannot be sold to satisfy a debt. These exemptions are set forth in the Federal Code but, in most cases, vary to some extent by state, because the states have the option to opt out of the federal exemption scheme.

**Forbearance:**   Where you enter into a payment plan with the bank where the arrearages (past due balance) are added to the end of the loan, and you pay a higher monthly payment for a period of time after which the bank reinstates your mortgage.

**Foreclosure sale:**   When you take out a mortgage to buy your house, the bank has a secured interest in the house for the amount of the loan. A foreclosure action is a lawsuit where the bank asks a judge to give your house to them to sell so that they can recover the outstanding balance of the loan.

**Future interest:**   An interest in real property to which you have no current right of possession, but which will arise in the future upon the occurrence of a specific event.

**Homestead:**   A debtor's primary residence that may be wholly or partially exempt from claims of creditors and bankruptcy trustees, under certain conditions and with exceptions.

**Judgment:**   Obtained by the creditor by suing you in court. If you have no defense other than "I can't pay," or if you fail to respond at all, you will lose and a judgment will be entered against you and the creditor can use it to garnish (take) your wages, bank accounts, place a lien against your real property, or even take your Rolex watch to satisfy (pay) the judgment.

**Judgment creditor:**   A creditor with unsecured debt who has sued you for default and obtained a judgment against you, thereby becoming a judgment creditor with the ability to force the sale of many of your assets, place a lien on your house, force you to show up to a debtor's examination and question you as to the whereabouts, of your assets, attach your business, your bank accounts, and garnish your wages in order to obtain the balance, plus late fees, interest, court costs, and attorneys fees owed them.

**Lien:**   A right to either force the owner of certain property (you) to liquidate (sell) that property so that the creditor can be payed the debt you owe to him. A lien can either be created by a creditor suing you in court for a judgment, a *judgment lien* or you may voluntarily have allowed a lien to be placed on the property as collateral for a loan.

**Nondischargeable debt:**   Debt that in all likelihood will not be discharged in bankruptcy court. These include, for example, child support, alimony, most student loans, most IRS debts, and other tax burdens judgments against you for personal injuries you have caused another, debts arising from fraud on your creditors (for example, using false information to get credit, charging with no reasonable expectation that you would ever be able to pay).

**Nonpurchase money secured debt:**   Credit obtained by putting collateral, such as a paid off car, as security to ensure repayment of the debt. A creditor holding a security interest in your property has the right to take the property in the event that you default on your payments (stop paying your bills when due).

**Purchase money secured debt:**   Credit that has been extended to you on the basis of the value of the property purchased.

**Reaffirmation agreement:**   An agreement to repay a debt either during your bankruptcy proceeding or afterwards, when due to your discharge (or pending discharge) in bankruptcy, you no longer have a legal obligation to pay. Often creditors will offer substantial savings in balance due and interest rates to encourage you to reaffirm the debt.

**Redemption:**   Often as a result of filing for bankruptcy, your secured creditors will offer you the opportunity to "redeem," that is, buy your secured property free and clear, and often at a greatly reduced price compared to the balance owed to them.

**Sale on the courthouse steps:**   Refers to weekly auctions of properties that have been the subject of a foreclosure, and often takes place right in the lobby of your local courthouse. At a sale on the courthouse steps, your home will probably be sold for far less than its fair market value. Investors will bid against the bank who may open with a bid as low as one hundred dollars. Investors may go up to and or exceed amount of mortgage. The bank has a credit for the amount of the mortgage and if the investors fail to bid up to the amount of the mortgage, the bank gets the house and will then sell it in a foreclosure sale.

**Tools of the trade:**   Items of personal property necessary for your employment.

**Unliquidated debt:**   A debt you and the creditor are aware of but, the exact amount of the debt has not been determined.

**Unsecured debt:**   Credit that has been extended to you only on your promise to repay it. Most unsecured debt is credit card debt, although, for example, in the case of a new car, with a large loan, often the minute you drive it off the lot and the value drops significantly, and a portion of the new car loan becomes unsecured.

### UNITED STATES BANKRUPTCY COURT

## NOTICE TO INDIVIDUAL CONSUMER DEBTOR(S)

The purpose of this notice is to acquaint you with the four chapters of the federal Bankruptcy Code under which you may file a bankruptcy petition. The bankruptcy law is complicated and not easily described. Therefore, you should seek the advice of an attorney to learn of your rights and responsibilities under the law should you decide to file a petition with the court. Neither the judge nor the court's employees may provide you with legal advice.

**Chapter 7: Liquidation ($155 filing fee plus $45 administrative fee)***

1. Chapter 7 is designed for debtors in financial difficulty who do not have the ability to pay their existing debts.

2. Under Chapter 7 a trustee takes possession of all your property. You may claim certain of your property as exempt under governing law. The trustee then liquidates the property and uses the proceeds to pay your creditors according to priorities of the Bankruptcy Code.

3. The purpose of filing a Chapter 7 case is to obtain a discharge of your existing debts. If, however, you are found to have committed certain kinds of improper conduct described in the Bankruptcy Code, your discharge may be denied by the court, and the purpose for which you filed the bankruptcy petition will be defeated.

4. Even if you receive a discharge, there are some debts that are not discharged under the law. Therefore, you may still be responsible for such debts as certain taxes and student loans, alimony and support payments, criminal restitution, and debts for death or personal injury caused by driving while intoxicated from alcohol or drugs.

5. Under certain circumstances you may keep property that you have purchased subject to a valid security interest. Your attorney can explain the options that are available to you.

**Chapter 13: Repayment of All or Part of the Debts of an Individual with Regular Income ($155 filing fee plus $30 administrative fee)***

1. Chapter 13 is designed for individuals with regular income who are temporarily unable to pay their debts but would like to pay them in installments over a period of time. You are only eligible for Chapter 13 if your debts do not exceed certain dollar amounts set forth in the Bankruptcy Code.

2. Under Chapter 13 you must file a plan with the court to repay your creditors all or part of the money that you owe them, using your future earnings. Usually the period allowed by the court to repay your debts is three years, but not more than five years. Your plan must be approved by the court before it can take effect.

3. Under Chapter 13, unlike Chapter 7, you may keep all your property, both exempt and non-exempt, as long as you continue to make payments under the plan.

4. After completion of payments under your plan, your debts are discharged except alimony and support payments, student loans, certain debts including criminal fines and restitution and debts for death or personal injury caused by driving while intoxicated from alcohol or drugs, and long term secured obligations.

**Chapter 11: Reorganization ($830 filing fee)***

Chapter 11 is designed primarily for the reorganization of a business but is also available to consumer debtors. Its provisions are quite complicated, and any decision for an individual to file a Chapter 11 petition should be reviewed with an attorney.

**Chapter 12: Family Farmer ($230 filing fee)***

Chapter 12 is designed to permit family farmers to repay their debts over a period of time from future earnings and is in many ways similar to a Chapter 13. The eligibility requirements are restrictive, limiting its use to those who income arises primarily from a family owned farm.

\* Fees are subject to change and should be confirmed before filing.

### ACKNOWLEDGEMENT

I, the debtor, affirm that I have read this notice.

_____
Case Number

11/25/02 _____    _____
Date      Deborah D. Debtor      Debtor      Joint Debtor, if any

**INSTRUCTIONS:** If the debtor is an individual, a copy of this notice personally signed by the debtor must accompany any bankruptcy petition filed with the Clerk. If filed by joint debtors, the notice must be personally signed by each. Failure to comply may result in the petition not being accepted for filing.

NOTICE TO INDIVIDUAL CONSUMER DEBTOR(S)      Copyright 1995 M. Mohr, Inc. [1-800-998-2424]

## NOTICE TO INDIVIDUAL CONSUMER DEBTOR(S)

(Official Form 1) (9/97)

| FORM B1 | United States Bankruptcy Court<br>Southern District of Florida | VOLUNTARY PETITION |
|---|---|---|

| Name of Debtor (If individual, enter Last, First, Middle):<br>Deborah D. Debtor | Name of Joint Debtor (Spouse)(Last, First, Middle) |
|---|---|
| All Other Names used by the Debtor in the last 6 years<br>(include married, maiden, and trade names): | All Other Names used by the Joint Debtor in the last 6 years<br>(include married, maiden, and trade names): |
| Soc.Sec./Tax I.D. No. (If more than one, state all):<br>107-20-2694 | Soc.Sec./Tax I.D. No. (If more than one, state all): |
| Street Address of Debtor (No. & Street, City, State & Zip Code):<br>2056 S.E. 117th Street<br>Pompano Beach, FL 33308 | Street Address of Joint Debtor (No. & Street, City, State & Zip Code): |
| County of Residence or of the<br>Principal Place of Business: Broward | County of Residence or of the<br>Principal Place of Business: |
| Mailing Address of Debtor (if different from street address): | Mailing Address of Joint Debtor (if different from street address): |

Location of Principal Assets of Business Debtor
(if different from street address above):

### Information Regarding the Debtor (Check the Applicable Boxes)

**Venue** (Check any applicable box)

☒ Debtor has been domiciled or has had a residence, principal place of business, or principal assets in this District for 180 days immediately preceding the date of this petition or for a longer part of such 180 days than in any other District.

☐ There is a bankruptcy case concerning debtor's affiliate, general partner, or partnership pending in this District.

| **Type of Debtor** (Check any applicable box) | | **Chapter or Section of Bankruptcy Code Under Which the Petition is Filed** (Check one box) | | |
|---|---|---|---|---|
| ☒ Individual(s) | ☐ Railroad | ☒ Chapter 7 | ☐ Chapter 11 | ☐ Chapter 13 |
| ☐ Corporation | ☐ Stockbroker | ☐ Chapter 9 | ☐ Chapter 12 | |
| ☐ Partnership | ☐ Commodity Broker | ☐ Sec. 304 - Case Ancillary to Foreign Proceeding | | |
| ☐ Other _____ | | | | |

**Nature of Debts** (Check one box)

☒ Consumer/Non-Business ☐ Business

**Chapter 11 Small Business** (Check all boxes that apply)

☐ Debtor is a small business as defined in 11 USC §101.

☐ Debtor is and elects to be considered a small business under 11 USC §1121(e)(Optional)

**Filing Fee** (Check one box)

☒ Full Filing Fee attached

☐ Filing Fee to be paid in installments. (Applicable to individuals only.) Must attach signed application for the court's consideration certifying that the debtor is unable to pay fee except in installments. Rule 1006(b). See Official Form No. 3.

**Statistical/Administrative Information (Estimates Only)**

☐ Debtor estimates that funds will be available for distribution to unsecured creditors.

☒ Debtor estimates that, after any exempt property is excluded and administrative expenses paid, there will be no funds available for distribution to unsecured creditors.

THIS SPACE IS FOR COURT USE ONLY

Estimated Number of Creditors

| 1-15 | 16-49 | 50-99 | 100-199 | 200-999 | 1000-over |
|---|---|---|---|---|---|
| ☒ | ☐ | ☐ | ☐ | ☐ | ☐ |

Estimated Assets

| $0 to<br>$50,000 | $50,001 to<br>$100,000 | $100,001 to<br>$500,000 | $500,001 to<br>$1 million | $1,000,001 to<br>$10 million | $10,000,001 to<br>$50 million | $50,000,001 to<br>$100 million | More than<br>$100 million |
|---|---|---|---|---|---|---|---|
| ☐ | ☐ | ☒ | ☐ | ☐ | ☐ | ☐ | ☐ |

Estimated Debts

| $0 to<br>$50,000 | $50,001 to<br>$100,000 | $100,001 to<br>$500,000 | $500,001 to<br>$1 million | $1,000,001 to<br>$10 million | $10,000,001 to<br>$50 million | $50,000,001 to<br>$100 million | More than<br>$100 million |
|---|---|---|---|---|---|---|---|
| ☐ | ☐ | ☒ | ☐ | ☐ | ☐ | ☐ | ☐ |

[BOF1p1] VOLUNTARY PETITION

Copyright 1997 M. Mohr, Inc. [1-800-998-2424]

## FORM B1—SIDE 1

(Official Form 1) (9/97)

| Voluntary Petition | FORM B1, Page 2 |
|---|---|
| *(This page must be completed and filed in every case)* | Name of Debtor(s): Deborah D. Debtor |

**Prior Bankruptcy Case Filed Within Last 6 Years (If more than one, attached additional sheet)**

| Location Where Filed: | Case Number: | Date: |
|---|---|---|

**Pending Bankruptcy Case Filed by any Spouse, Partner or Affiliate of this Debtor (If more than one, attached additional sheet)**

| Name of Debtor: | Case Number: | Date: |
|---|---|---|
| Relationship: | District: | Judge: |

## Signatures

### Signature(s) of Debtor(s) (Individual/Joint)

I declare under penalty of perjury that the information provided in this petition is true and correct.
[If petitioner is an individual whose debts are primarily consumer debts and has chosen to file under Chapter 7] I am aware that I may proceed under chapter 7, 11, 12 or 13 of title 11, United States Code, understand the relief available under each such chapter, and choose to proceed under chapter 7.
I request relief in accordance with the chapter of title 11, United States Code, specified in this petition.

X_____
Signature of Debtor Deborah D. Debtor

X_____
Signature of Joint Debtor

_____
Telephone Number (if not represented by attorney)

November 25, 2002
Date

### Signature of Debtor (Corporation/Partnership)

I declare under penalty of perjury that the information provided in this petition if true and correct, and that I have been authorized to file this petition on behalf of the debtor.

The debtor requests relief in accordance with the chapter of title 11, United States Code, specified in this petition.

X_____
Signature of Authorized Individual

_____
Printed Name of Authorized Individual

_____
Title of Authorized Individual

_____
Date

### Signature of Attorney

X_____
Signature of Attorney for Debtor(s)

_____
Printed Name of Attorney for Debtor(s)

_____
Firm Name

_____
Address

_____
Telephone Number

_____
Date

### Exhibit A

(To be completed if debtor is required to file periodic reports (e.g., forms 10K and 10Q) with the Securities and Exchange Commission pursuant to Section 13 or 15(d) of the Securities Exchange Act of 1934 and is requesting relief under chapter 11.)

☐ Exhibit A is attached and made a part of this petition.

### Exhibit B

(To be completed if debtor is an individual whose debts are primarily consumer debts)
I, the attorney for the petitioner named in the foregoing petition, declare that I have informed the petitioner that [he or she] may proceed under chapter 7, 11, 12 or 13 of title 11, United States Code, and have explained the relief available under each such chapter.

X_____ 11/25/02
Signature of Attorney for Debtor(s)     Date

### Signature of Non-Attorney Petition Preparer

I certify that I am a bankruptcy petition preparer as defined in 11 U.S.C. §110, that I prepared this document for compensation, and that I have provided the debtor with a copy of this document.

_____
Printed or Typed Name of Bankruptcy Petition Preparer

_____
Social Security Number

_____
Address

Names and Social Security numbers of all other individuals who prepared or assisted in preparing this document: If more than one person prepared this document, attach additional signed sheets conforming to the appropriate official form for each person.

X_____
Signature of Bankruptcy Petition Preparer

_____
Date

A bankruptcy petition preparer's failure to comply with the provisions of title 11 and the Federal Rules of Bankruptcy may result in fines or imprisonment or both. 11 U.S.C. §110; 18 U.S.C. §156.

[BOF1p2] VOLUNTARY PETITION     Copyright 1997 M. Mohr, Inc. [1-800-998-2424]

## FORM B1—SIDE 2

Form B6
(6/90)

## FORMS 6.  SCHEDULES

Summary of Schedules

Schedule A - Real Property
Schedule B - Personal Property
Schedule C - Property Claimed as Exempt
Schedule D - Creditors Holding Secured Claims
Schedule E - Creditors Holding Unsecured Priority Claims
Schedule F - Creditors Holding Unsecured Nonpriority Claims
Schedule G - Executory Contracts and Unexpired Leases
Schedule H - Codebtors
Schedule I - Current Income of Individual Debtor(s)
Schedule J - Current Expenditures of Individual Debtor(s)

Unsworn Declaration under Penalty of Perjury

GENERAL INSTRUCTIONS: The first page of the debtor's schedules and the first page of any amendments thereto must contain a caption as in Form 16B. Subsequent pages should be identified with the debtor's name and case number. If the schedules are filed with the petition, the case number should be left blank.

Schedules D, E, and F have been designed for the listing of each claim only once. Even when a claim is secured only in part or entitled to priority only in part, it still should be listed only once. A claim which is secured in whole or in part should be listed on Schedule D only, and a claim which is entitled to priority in whole or in part should be listed on Schedule E only. Do not list the same claim twice. If a creditor has more than one claim, such as claims arising from separate transactions, each claim should be scheduled separately.

Review the specific instructions for each schedule before completing the schedule.

### FORM B6: SUMMARY OF SCHEDULES

**United States Bankruptcy Court**
**Southern District of Florida**

IN RE

Deborah D. Debtor
107-20-2694

2056 S.E. 117th Street                                   Case No. _____
Pompano Beach, FL  33308

                                        **DEBTOR(S)**      Chapter _7_____

## SUMMARY OF SCHEDULES

Indicate as to each schedule whether that schedule is attached and state the number of pages in each.  Report the totals from Schedules A, B, D, E, F, I, and J in the boxes provided.  Add the amounts from Schedules A and B to determine the total amount of the debtor's assets.  Add the amounts from Schedules D, E, and F to determine the total amount of the debtor's liabilities.

AMOUNTS SCHEDULED

| | NAME OF SCHEDULE | ATTACHED (YES/NO) | NUMBER OF SHEETS | ASSETS | LIABILITIES | OTHER |
|---|---|---|---|---|---|---|
| A | Real Property | Yes | 1 | 112,000.00 | | |
| B | Personal Property | Yes | 4 | 16,196.00 | | |
| C | Property Claimed as Exempt | Yes | 1 | | | |
| D | Creditors Holding Secured Claims | Yes | 1 | | 103,228.00 | |
| E | Creditors Holding Unsecured Priority Claims | Yes | 1 | | 0.00 | |
| F | Creditors Holding Unsecured Nonpriority Claims | Yes | 3 | | 51,761.27 | |
| G | Executory Contracts and Unexpired Leases | Yes | 1 | | | |
| H | Codebtors | Yes | 1 | | | |
| I | Current Income of Individual Debtor(s) | Yes | 1 | | | 1,900.00 |
| J | Current Expenditures of Individual Debtor(s) | Yes | 1 | | | 1,962.00 |
| | **Total Number of Sheets of All Schedules** | | 15 | | | |
| | **Total Assets** | | | 128,196.00 | | |
| | **Total Liabilities** | | | | 154,989.27 | |

IN RE <u>Deborah D. Debtor</u>                     Case No. _____

Debtor(s)

## SCHEDULE A - REAL PROPERTY

Except as directed below, list all real property in which the debtor has any legal, equitable, or future interest, including all property owned as a co-tenant, community property, or in which the debtor has a life estate. Include any property in which the debtor holds rights and powers exercisable for the debtor's own benefit. If the debtor is married, state whether husband, wife, or both own the property by placing an "H" for Husband, "W" for Wife, "J" for Joint, or "C" for Community in the column labeled "HWJC." If the debtor holds no interest in real property, write "None" under "Description and Location of Property".

Do not include interests in executory contracts and unexpired leases on the schedule. List them in Schedule G - Executory Contracts and Unexpired Leases.

If an entity claims to have a lien or hold a security interest in any property, state the amount of the secured claim. See Schedule D. If no entity claims to hold a secured interest in the property, write "None" in the column labeled "Amount of Secured Claim".

If the debtor is an individual or if a joint petition is filed, state the amount of any exemption claimed in the property only in Schedule C - Property Claimed as Exempt.

| DESCRIPTION AND LOCATION OF PROPERTY | NATURE OF DEBTOR'S INTEREST IN PROPERTY | H W J C | CURRENT MARKET VALUE OF DEBTOR'S INTEREST IN PROPERTY WITHOUT DEDUCTING ANY SECURED CLAIM OR EXEMPTION | AMOUNT OF SECURED CLAIM |
|---|---|---|---|---|
| Debtor's Homestead Real Property located at 2056 S.E. 117th Street, Pompano Beach, FL 33308 and legally described as Pasta Vista First Add Rev 32-44 B, Lot 7, Blk 40 | Solely owned | | 112,000.00 | 89,000.00 |
| | | TOTAL | 112,000.00 | |

(Report also on Summary of Schedules)

[BOF6A] SCHEDULE A - REAL PROPERTY                     Copyright 1993 M. Mohr, Inc. [1-800-998-2424]

## FORM B6A: SCHEDULE A—REAL PROPERTY

IN RE Deborah D. Debtor
Debtor(s)

Case No. _____

## SCHEDULE B - PERSONAL PROPERTY

Except as directed below, list all personal property of the debtor of whatever kind. If the debtor has no property in one or more of the categories, place an "X" in the appropriate position in the column labeled "None". If additional space is needed in any category, attached a separate sheet properly identified with the case name, case number, and the number of the category. If the debtor is married, state whether husband, wife, or both own the property by placing an "H" for Husband, "W" for Wife, "J" for Joint, or "C" for Community in the column labeled "HWJC." If the debtor is an individual or a joint petition is filed, state the amount of any exemptions only in Schedule C - Property Claimed as Exempt.

Do not include interests in executory contracts and unexpired leases on the schedule. List them in Schedule G - Executory Contracts and Unexpired Leases.

If the property is being held for the debtor by someone else, state that person's name and address under "Description and Location of Property".

| TYPE OF PROPERTY | N O N E | DESCRIPTION AND LOCATION OF PROPERTY | H W J C | CURRENT MARKET VALUE OF DEBTOR'S INTEREST IN PROPERTY WITHOUT DEDUCTING ANY SECURED CLAIM OR EXEMPTION |
|---|---|---|---|---|
| 1. Cash on hand. | | cash on hand | | 15.00 |
| 2. Checking, savings or other financial accounts, certificates of deposit, or shares in banks, savings and loan, thrift, building and loan, and homestead associations, or credit unions, brokerage houses, or cooperatives. | | Southtrust Bank Checking account | | 46.00 |
| 3. Security deposits with public utilities, telephone companies, landlords, and others. | X | | | |
| 4. Household goods and furnishings, include audio, video, and computer equipment. | | Debtor's household goods and furnishings:  living room and family room, 2 sofas,  chairs, bookcases, desk, lamps $190.00; bedrooms, 1 single bed, 1 double bed mattress, 4 chests $100.00; patio furniture $10.00; dinette table and chairs $20.00; refridgerator $100.00, stove $50.00, dishwasher $50.00, washer $100.00, dryer $20.00, microwave $15.00, television $20.00, vcr $10.00. | | 680.00 |
| 5. Books, pictures and other art objects, antiques, stamp, coin, record, tape, compact disc, and other collections or collectibles. | | debtor's books, pictures and other art objects | | 20.00 |
| 6. Wearing apparel. | | debtor's clothing and accessories | | 75.00 |

[BOF6B] SCHEDULE B - PERSONAL PROPERTY

## FORM B6B: SCHEDULE B—PERSONAL PROPERTY

IN RE Deborah D. Debtor                                        Case No. _____

_Debtor(s)_

## SCHEDULE B - PERSONAL PROPERTY (Continuation Sheet)

| TYPE OF PROPERTY | N O N E | DESCRIPTION AND LOCATION OF PROPERTY | H W J C | CURRENT MARKET VALUE OF DEBTOR'S INTEREST IN PROPERTY WITHOUT DEDUCTING ANY SECURED CLAIM OR EXEMPTION |
|---|---|---|---|---|
| 7. Furs and jewelry. | X | | | |
| 8. Firearms and sports, photographic, and other hobby equipment. | X | | | |
| 9. Interest in insurance policies. Name insurance company of each policy and itemize surrender or refund value of each. | X | | | |
| 10. Annuities. Itemize and name each issue. | X | | | |
| 11. Interests in IRA, ERISA, Keogh, or other pension or profit sharing plans. Itemize. | X | | | |
| 12. Stock and interests in incorporated and unincorporated businesses. Itemize. | X | | | |
| 13. Interests in partnerships or joint ventures. Itemize. | X | | | |
| 14. Government and corporate bonds and other negotiable and non-negotiable instruments. | X | | | |
| 15. Accounts receivable. | X | | | |
| 16. Alimony, maintenance, support, and property settlements in which the debtor is or may be entitled. Give particulars. | X | | | |

[BOF6Bc] SCHEDULE B - PERSONAL PROPERTY (Continuation Sheet)           Copyright 1993 M. Mohr, Inc. [1-800-998-2424]

IN RE <u>Deborah D. Debtor</u>                                                 Case No. _____
Debtor(s)

## SCHEDULE B - PERSONAL PROPERTY (Continuation Sheet)

| TYPE OF PROPERTY | N O N E | DESCRIPTION AND LOCATION OF PROPERTY | H W J C | CURRENT MARKET VALUE OF DEBTOR'S INTEREST IN PROPERTY WITHOUT DEDUCTING ANY SECURED CLAIM OR EXEMPTION |
|---|---|---|---|---|
| 17. Other liquidated debts owing debtor including tax refunds. Give particulars. | X | | | |
| 18. Equitable or future interest, life estates, and rights or powers exercisable for the benefit of the debtor other than those listed in Schedule of Real Property. | X | | | |
| 19. Contingent and noncontingent interests in estate of a decedent, death benefit plan, life insurance policy, or trust. | X | | | |
| 20. Other contingent and unliquidated claims of every nature, including tax refunds, counterclaims of the debtor, and rights to setoff claims. Give estimated value of each. | X | | | |
| 21. Patents, copyrights, and other intellectual property. Give particulars. | X | | | |
| 22. Licenses, franchises, and other general intangibles. Give particulars. | X | | | |
| 23. Automobiles, trucks, trailers, and other vehicles and accessories. | | debtor's 2000 American Va-Zoom Automobile, VIN 5A4R CO2 1224 3345 XYZ | | 15,360.00 |
| 24. Boats, motors, and accessories. | X | | | |
| 25. Aircraft and accessories. | X | | | |

IN RE Deborah D. Debtor                                    Case No. _____

                    Debtor(s)

## SCHEDULE B - PERSONAL PROPERTY (Continuation Sheet)

| TYPE OF PROPERTY | N O N E | DESCRIPTION AND LOCATION OF PROPERTY | H W J C | CURRENT MARKET VALUE OF DEBTOR'S INTEREST IN PROPERTY WITHOUT DEDUCTING ANY SECURED CLAIM OR EXEMPTION |
|---|---|---|---|---|
| 26. Office equipment, furnishings, and supplies. | X | | | |
| 27. Machinery, fixtures, equipment, and supplies used in business. | X | | | |
| 28. Inventory. | X | | | |
| 29. Animals. | X | | | |
| 30. Crops - growing or harvested. Give particulars. | X | | | |
| 31. Farming equipment and implements. | X | | | |
| 32. Farm supplies, chemicals, and feed. | X | | | |
| 33. Other personal property of any kind not already listed, such as season tickets. Itemize. | X | | | |
| | | | TOTAL | 16,196.00 |

(Include amounts from any continuation sheets attached. Report total also on Summary of Schedules.)

_____ 0 continuation sheets attached

[BOF6Bc] SCHEDULE B - PERSONAL PROPERTY (Continuation Sheet)

IN RE Deborah D. Debtor _____    Case No. _____
                    Debtor(s)

## SCHEDULE C - PROPERTY CLAIMED AS EXEMPT

Debtor elects the exemptions to which debtor is entitled under:

(Check one box)

☐ 11 U.S.C. § 522(b)(1): Exemptions provided in 11 U.S.C. § 522(d).  Note:  These exemptions are available only in certain states.

☒ 11 U.S.C. § 522(b)(2): Exemptions available under applicable nonbankruptcy federal laws, state or local law where the debtor's domicile has been
               located for 180 immediately preceding the filing of the petition, or for a longer portion of the 180-day period than in any other
               place, and the debtor's interest as a tenant by the entirety or joint tenant to the extent the interest is exempt from process
               under applicable nonbankruptcy law.

| DESCRIPTION OF PROPERTY | SPECIFY LAW PROVIDING EACH EXEMPTION | VALUE OF CLAIMED EXEMPTION | CURRENT MARKET VALUE OF PROPERTY WITHOUT DEDUCTING EXEMPTIONS |
|---|---|---|---|
| Real Property | | | |
| Debtor's Homestead Real Property located at 2056 S.E. 117th Street, Pompano Beach, FL 33308 and legally described as Pasta Vista First Add Rev 32-44 B, Lot 7, Blk 40    FSA 222.05, Const. 10-4 | | 112,000.00 | 112,000.00 |
| Cash on hand | | | |
| cash on hand    Constitution 10-4 | | 15.00 | 15.00 |
| Checking, savings or other financial accounts | | | |
| Southtrust Bank Checking Constitution 10-4 account | | 46.00 | 46.00 |
| Household goods and furnishings | | | |
| Debtor's household goods Constitution 10-4 and furnishi | | 680.00 | 680.00 |
| Books, pictures and other art objects | | | |
| debtor's books, pictures Constitution 10-4 and other ar | | 20.00 | 20.00 |
| Wearing apparel | | | |
| debtor's clothing and    Constitution 10-4 accessories | | 75.00 | 75.00 |
| Automobiles, trucks, trailers, and other vehicles | | | |
| debtor's 2000 American    Constitution 10-4 Va-Zoom Autom | | 1,000.00 | 15,360.00 |

[BOF6C] SCHEDULE C - PROPERTY CLAIMED AS EXEMPT

## FORM B6C: SCHEDULE C—PROPERTY CLAIMED AS EXEMPT

IN RE Deborah D. Debtor                                    Case No. _____

Debtor(s)

## SCHEDULE D - CREDITORS HOLDING SECURED CLAIMS

State the name, mailing address, including zip code, and account number, if any, of all entities holding claims secured by property of the debtor as of the date of filing of the petition. List creditors holding all types of secured interests such as judgment liens, garnishments, statutory liens, mortgages, deeds of trust, and other security interests. List creditors in alphabetical order to the extent practicable. If all secured creditors will not fit on this page, use the continuation sheet provided.

If any entity other than a spouse in a joint case may be jointly liable on a claim, place an "X" in the column labeled "Codebtor", include the entity on the appropriate schedule of creditors, and complete Schedule H - Codebtors. If a joint petition is filed, state whether husband, wife, both of them, or the marital community may be liable on each claim by placing an "H","W","J", or "C", respectively, in the column labeled "HWJC."

If the claim is contingent, place an "X" in the column labeled "Contingent". If the claim is unliquidated, place an "X" in the column labeled "Unliquidated". If the claim is disputed, place an "X" in the column labeled "Disputed". (You may need to place an "X" in more than one of these three columns.)

Report the total of all claims listed on this schedule in the box labeled "Total" on the last sheet of the completed schedule. Report this total also on the Summary of Schedules.

☐ Check this box if debtor has no creditors holding secured claims to report on this Schedule D.

| CREDITOR'S NAME AND MAILING ADDRESS INCLUDING ZIP CODE | CODEBTOR | HWJC | DATE CLAIM WAS INCURRED NATURE OF LIEN AND DESCRIPTION AND MARKET VALUE OF PROPERTY SUBJECT TO LIEN | CONTINGENT | UNLIQUIDATED | DISPUTED | AMOUNT OF CLAIM WITHOUT DEDUCTING VALUE OF COLLATERAL | UNSECURED PORTION, IF ANY |
|---|---|---|---|---|---|---|---|---|
| ACCOUNT NO. 908765431<br><br>American Auto Retailers<br>1000 CarLoan Way<br>Fort Lauderdale, FL 33305 | | | 2000.  Loan on Debtor's American Va-Zoom Automobile<br><br>Value $ | | | | 14,228.00 | |
| ACCOUNT NO. 112233-4455-99<br><br>Pompano National Mortgage<br>112 North Atlantic Ave<br>Pompano, FL 33211 | | | 1996 mortgage loan on debtor's homestead real property<br><br>Value $     112,000.00 | | | | 89,000.00 | |
| ACCOUNT NO.<br><br><br><br>Value $ | | | | | | | | |
| ACCOUNT NO.<br><br><br><br>Value $ | | | | | | | | |

_____ 0 Continuation Sheets attached

| | Subtotal (Total of this page) | 103,228.00 |
|---|---|---|
| (Complete only on last sheet of Schedule D) | **TOTAL** | 103,228.00 |

(Report total also on Summary of Schedules)

## FORM B6D: SCHEDULE D—CREDITORS HOLDING SECURED CLAIMS

IN RE <u>Deborah D. Debtor</u>                                    Case No. _____
                    Debtor(s)

## SCHEDULE E - CREDITORS HOLDING UNSECURED PRIORITY CLAIMS

A complete list of claims entitled to priority, listed separately by type of priority, is to be set forth on the sheets provided. Only holders of unsecured claims entitled to priority should be listed in this schedule. In the boxes provided on the attached sheets, state the name and mailing address, including zip code, and account number if any, of all entities holding priority claims against the debtor or the property of the debtor, as of the date of the filing of this petition.

If any entity other than a spouse in a joint case may be jointly liable on a claim, place an "X" in the column labeled "Codebtor", include the entity on the appropriate schedule of creditors, and complete Schedule H - Codebtors. If a joint petition is filed, state whether husband, wife, both of them, or the marital community may be liable on each claim by placing an "H","W","J", or "C", respectively, in the column labeled "HWJC."

If the claim is contingent, place an "X" in the column labeled "Contingent". If the claim is unliquidated, place an "X" in the column labeled "Unliquidated". If the claim is disputed, place an "X" in the column labeled "Disputed". (You may need to place an "X" in more than one of these three columns.)

Report the total of claims listed on each sheet in the box labeled "Subtotal" on each sheet. Report the Total of all claims listed on this Schedule E in the box labeled "Total" on the last sheet of the completed schedule. Repeat this total also on the Summary of Schedules.

☒ Check this box if debtor has no creditors holding unsecured priority claims to report on this Schedule E.

**TYPES OF PRIORITY CLAIMS** (Check the appropriate box(es) below if claims in that category are listed on the attached sheets)

☐ **Extensions of credit in an involuntary case**
Claims arising in the ordinary course of the debtor's business or financial affairs after the commencement of the case but before the earlier of the appointment of a trustee or the order for relief. 11 U.S.C. §507(a)(2)

☐ **Wages, salaries, and commissions**
Wages, salaries, and commissions, including vacation, severance, and sick leave pay owing to employees and commissions owing to qualifying independent sales representatives up to $4300* per person earned within 90 days immediately preceding the filing of the original petition, or the cessation of business, whichever occurred first, to the extent provided in 11 U.S.C. §507(a)(3).

☐ **Contributions to employee benefit plans**
Money owed to employee benefit plans for services rendered within 180 days immediately preceding the filing of the original petition, or the cessation of business, whichever occurred first, to the extent provided in 11 U.S.C. §507(a)(4).

☐ **Certain farmers and fishermen**
Claims of certain farmers and fishermen, up to a maximum of $4300* per farmer or fisherman, against the debtor, as provided in 11 U.S.C. §507(a)(5).

☐ **Deposits by individuals**
Claims of individuals up to a maximum of $1,950* for deposits for the purchase, lease, or rental of property or services for personal, family, or household use, that were not delivered or provided. 11 U.S.C. §507(a)(6)

☐ **Alimony, Maintenance, or Support**
Claims of a spouse, former spouse, or child of the debtor for alimony, maintenance, or support, to the extent provided in 11 U.S.C. § 507(a)(7).

☐ **Taxes and Other Certain Debts Owed to Governmental Units**
Taxes, customs duties, and penalties owing to federal, state, and local governmental units as set forth in 11 U.S.C. §507(a)(8).

☐ **Commitments to Maintain the Capital of an Insured Depository Institution**
Claims based on commitments to the FDIC, RTC, Director of the Office of Thrift Supervision, Comptroller of the Currency, or Board of Governors of the Federal Reserve System, or their predecessors or successors, to maintain the capital of an insured depository institution. 11 U.S.C. §507(a)(9).

* Amounts are subject to adjustment on April 1, 2001, and every three years thereafter with respect to cases commenced on or after the date of adjustment.

_____ Continuation Sheets attached

[BOF6Ep1] SCHEDULE E - CREDITORS HOLDING UNSECURED PRIORITY CLAIMS                    Copyright 1998 M. Mohr, Inc. [1-800-998-2424]

## FORM B6E: SCHEDULE E—CREDITORS HOLDING UNSECURED PRIORITY CLAIMS

IN RE <u>Deborah D. Debtor</u>          Case No. _____
Debtor(s)

## SCHEDULE F - CREDITORS HOLDING UNSECURED NONPRIORITY CLAIMS

State the name, mailing address, including zip code, and account number, if any, of all entities holding unsecured claims without priority against the debtor or the property of the debtor, as of the date of filing of the petition. Do not include claims listed in Schedules D and E. If all creditors will not fit on this page, use the continuation sheet provided.

If any entity other than a spouse in a joint case may be jointly liable on a claim, place an "X" in the column labeled "Codebtor", include the entity on the appropriate schedule of creditors, and complete Schedule H - Codebtors. If a joint petition is filed, state whether husband, wife, both of them, or the marital community may be liable on each claim by placing an "H","W","J", or "C", respectively, in the column labeled "HWJC."

If the claim is contingent, place an "X" in the column labeled "Contingent". If the claim is unliquidated, place an "X" in the column labeled "Unliquidated". If the claim is disputed, place an "X" in the column labeled "Disputed". (You may need to place an "X" in more than one of these three columns.)

Report total of all claims listed on this schedule in the box labeled "Total" on the last sheet of the completed schedule. Report this total also on the Summary of Schedules.

☐ Check this box if debtor has no creditors holding unsecured nonpriority claims to report on this Schedule F.

| CREDITOR'S NAME AND MAILING ADDRESS INCLUDING ZIP CODE | CODEBTOR | HWJC | DATE CLAIM WAS INCURRED AND CONSIDERATION FOR CLAIM IF CLAIM IS SUBJECT TO SETOFF, SO STATE | CONTINGENT | UNLIQUIDATED | DISPUTED | AMOUNT OF CLAIM |
|---|---|---|---|---|---|---|---|
| ACCOUNT NO.908 6543 211<br><br>Cell Phones Unlimited<br>32 N.W. 132 Street<br>Ft. Lauderdale,, FL 33305 | | | telephone charges | | | | 1,250.00 |
| ACCOUNT NO.<br><br>Credit Collectors<br>123 Paxel Way<br>Pompano Beach, FL 33099 | | | Assignee or other notification for:<br>Cell Phones Unlimited | | | | |
| ACCOUNT NO.9807 6543 8907 6543<br><br>Discover<br>PO Box 9088<br>Phoenix, TX 85033-9088 | | | various dates, miscellaneous consumer credit card purchases. | | | | 9,600.00 |
| ACCOUNT NO.<br><br>Clammy Collector, Esq.<br>999 Grabbit Way<br>Miami, FL 33168 | | | Assignee or other notification for:<br>Discover | | | | |

<u>     2</u> Continuation Sheets attached

Subtotal (Total of this page)    10,850.00

(Complete only on last sheet of Schedule F)   **TOTAL**

(Report total also on Summary of Schedules)

[BOF6Fp1] SCHEDULE F - CREDITORS HOLDING UNSECURED NONPRIORITY CLAIMS          Copyright 1993 M. Mohr, Inc. [1-800-998-2424]

## FORM B6F: SCHEDULE F—CREDITORS HOLDING UNSECURED NONPRIORITY CLAIMS

IN RE Deborah D. Debtor _____    Case No. _____
                              Debtor(s)

## SCHEDULE F - CREDITORS HOLDING UNSECURED NONPRIORITY CLAIMS
### (Continuation Sheet)

| CREDITOR'S NAME AND MAILING ADDRESS INCLUDING ZIP CODE | CODEBTOR | HWJC | DATE CLAIM WAS INCURRED AND CONSIDERATION FOR CLAIM IF CLAIM IS SUBJECT TO SETOFF, SO STATE | CONTINGENT | UNLIQUIDATED | DISPUTED | AMOUNT OF CLAIM |
|---|---|---|---|---|---|---|---|
| ACCOUNT NO. 999765 <br> Drs. Helliard & Cuttum <br> 1223 Buzzsaw Lane <br> Weston, FL 33455 | | | | | | | Unknown |
| ACCOUNT NO. 999-0765 <br> Large Department Store <br> 111 Department Store Way <br> Westin, FL 33022 | | | various, consumer credit card purchases | | | | 5,201.27 |
| ACCOUNT NO. 90 8765 4321 <br> Sears Premier Card <br> Payment Center Annex <br> 86 Annex <br> Eastridge, GA 30789-0001 | | | various dates. miscellaneous consumer credit card purchases at Sears | | | | 4,900.00 |
| ACCOUNT NO. <br> Alternative Risk Mgemt <br> 12 Buspar Way <br> Mt. Rushmore, IL 907666 | | | Assignee or other notification for: Sears Premier Card | | | | |
| ACCOUNT NO. 0987699000001 <br> Whalersville Emergency Phys <br> 966 Bottomfeeders Way <br> Whalersville, FL 33089 | | | 6/13/00 emergency room treatment and hosptital treatment, NCO | | | | 16,400.00 |

Sheet ____1____ of ____2____ Continuation Sheets attached to Schedule F

Subtotal (Total of this page)   26,501.27

(Complete only on last sheet of Schedule F)   **TOTAL**

(Report total also on Summary of Schedules)

[BOF6Fp2] SCHEDULE F - CREDITORS HOLDING UNSECURED NONPRIORITY CLAIMS (Continuation Sheet)          Copyright 1993 M. Mohr, Inc. [1-800-998-2424]

IN RE Deborah D. Debtor _____ Case No. _____
                        Debtor(s)

## SCHEDULE F - CREDITORS HOLDING UNSECURED NONPRIORITY CLAIMS
### (Continuation Sheet)

| CREDITOR'S NAME AND MAILING ADDRESS INCLUDING ZIP CODE | C O D E B T O R | H W J C | DATE CLAIM WAS INCURRED AND CONSIDERATION FOR CLAIM IF CLAIM IS SUBJECT TO SETOFF, SO STATE | C O N T I N G E N T | U N L I Q U I D A T E D | D I S P U T E D | AMOUNT OF CLAIM |
|---|---|---|---|---|---|---|---|
| ACCOUNT NO. Med Collectors, Inc 100 Sludgebuckets Road Pittsburgh, PA 09988 | | | Assignee or other notification for: Whalersville Emergency Ph | | | | |
| ACCOUNT NO. Whalersville Hospital 999 Bottomfeeders Way Whalersville, FL 33456 | | | 6-13-00 through 6-16-00 hosptital stay | | | | 14,410.00 |
| ACCOUNT NO. | | | | | | | |
| ACCOUNT NO. | | | | | | | |
| ACCOUNT NO. | | | | | | | |

Sheet _____2 of _____2 Continuation Sheets attached to Schedule F

Subtotal (Total of this page) | 14,410.00

(Complete only on last sheet of Schedule F) **TOTAL** | 51,761.27

(Report total also on Summary of Schedules)

IN RE <u>Deborah D. Debtor</u>                          Case No. _____

Debtor(s)

## SCHEDULE G - EXECUTORY CONTRACTS AND UNEXPIRED LEASES

Describe all executory contracts of any nature and all unexpired leases of real or personal property.  Include any timeshare interests.

State nature of debtor's interest in contract, i.e., "Purchaser", "Agent", etc.  State whether debtor is the lessor or lessee of a lease.

Provide the names and complete addresses of all other parties to each lease or contract described.

**NOTE:** A party listed on this schedule will not receive notice of the filing of this case unless the party is also scheduled in the appropriate schedule of creditors.

☒ Check this box if debtor has no executory contracts or unexpired leases.

| NAME AND MAILING ADDRESS, INCLUDING ZIP CODE, OF OTHER PARTIES TO LEASE OR CONTRACT | DESCRIPTION OF CONTRACT OR LEASE AND NATURE OF DEBTOR'S INTEREST.  STATE WHETHER LEASE IS FOR NONRESIDENTIAL REAL PROPERTY.  STATE CONTRACT NUMBER OF ANY GOVERNMENT CONTRACT. |
|---|---|
| | |

[BOF6G] SCHEDULE G - EXECUTORY CONTRACTS AND UNEXPIRED LEASES         

## FORM B6G: SCHEDULE G—EXECUTORY CONTRACTS AND UNEXPIRED LEASES

**IN RE** <u>Deborah D. Debtor</u>                                                                                      **Case No.** _____

Debtor(s)

## SCHEDULE H - CODEBTORS

Provide the information requested concerning any person or entity, other than a spouse in a joint case, that is also liable on any debts listed by debtor in the schedules of creditors. Include all guarantors and co-signers. In community property states, a married debtor not filing a joint case should report the name and address of the nondebtor spouse on this schedule. Include all names used by the nondebtor spouse during the six years immediately preceding the commencement of this case.

☒ Check this box if debtor has no codebtors.

| NAME AND ADDRESS OF CODEBTOR | NAME AND ADDRESS OF CREDITOR |
|---|---|
|  |  |

[BOF6H] SCHEDULE H - CODEBTORS                                                            Copyright 1993 M. Mohr, Inc. [1-800-998-2424]

## FORM B6H: SCHEDULE H—CODEBTORS

IN RE <u>Deborah D. Debtor</u>                                         Case No. _____
                          Debtor(s)

## SCHEDULE I - CURRENT INCOME OF INDIVIDUAL DEBTOR(S)

The column labeled "Spouse" must be completed in all cases filed by joint debtors and by a married debtor in a chapter 12 or 13 case whether or not a joint petition is filed, unless the spouses are separated and a joint petition is not filed.

| Debtor's Marital Status | DEPENDENTS OF DEBTOR AND SPOUSE | | | |
|---|---|---|---|---|
| | NAMES | | AGE | RELATIONSHIP |
| Divorced | | | | |

| Employment: | DEBTOR | SPOUSE |
|---|---|---|
| Occupation | Hair Dresser | |
| Name of Employer | Self | |
| How long employed | 10 Years | |
| Address of Employer | 2056 S.E. 117st. Street | |

|  | DEBTOR | SPOUSE |
|---|---|---|
| Income: (Estimate of average monthly income) | | |
| Current monthly gross wages, salary, and commissions (pro rate if not paid monthly) | $ 2,000.00 | $ |
| Estimated monthly overtime | $ | $ |
| **SUBTOTAL** | $ 2,000.00 | $ |
| LESS PAYROLL DEDUCTIONS | | |
|   a. Payroll taxes and Social Security | $ 300.00 | $ |
|   b. Insurance | $ | $ |
|   c. Union dues | $ | $ |
|   d. Other (Specify) _____ | $ | $ |
|   | $ | $ |
| **SUBTOTAL OF PAYROLL DEDUCTIONS** | $ 300.00 | $ |
| **TOTAL NET MONTHLY TAKE HOME PAY** | $ 1,700.00 | $ |
| Regular income from operation of business or profession or farm (attach detailed statement) | $ | $ |
| Income from real property | $ | $ |
| Interest and dividends | $ | $ |
| Alimony, maintenance or support payments payable to the debtor for the debtor's use or that of dependents listed above | $ | $ |
| Social Security or other government assistance Specify _____ | $ | $ |
| Other monthly income Specify Gifts from mother, Mary Debtor | $ 200.00 | $ |
|   | $ | $ |
|   | $ | $ |
| **TOTAL MONTHLY INCOME** | $ 1,900.00 | $ |

**TOTAL COMBINED MONTHLY INCOME**    $   1,900.00            (Report also on Summary of Schedules)

Describe any increase or decrease of more than 10% in any of the above categories anticipated to occur within the year following the filing of this document:

None

Copyright 1993 M. Mohr, Inc. [1-800-998-2424]

## FORM B6I: SCHEDULE I—CURRENT INCOME OF INDIVIDUAL DEBTOR(S)

IN RE Deborah D. Debtor _____     Case No. _____

             Debtor(s)

## SCHEDULE J - CURRENT EXPENDITURES OF INDIVIDUAL DEBTOR(S)

Complete this schedule by estimating the average monthly expenses of the debtor and the debtor's family.  Prorate any payments made bi-weekly, quarterly, semi-annually, or annually to show monthly rate.

☐ Check this box if a joint petition is filed and debtor's spouse maintains a separate household.  Complete a separate schedule of expenditures labeled "Spouse".

| | |
|---|---:|
| Rent or home mortgage payment (include lot rented for mobile home) | $ 760.00 |
| Are real estate taxes included?  Yes _X_  No _____ | |
| Is property insurance included?  Yes _X_  No _____ | |
| Utilities:  Electricity and heating fuel | $ 95.00 |
|         Water and sewer | $ 75.00 |
|         Telephone | $ 65.00 |
|         Other _____ | $ |
| Home maintenance (repairs and upkeep) | $ 30.00 |
| Food | $ 200.00 |
| Clothing | $ 30.00 |
| Laundry and dry cleaning | $ 25.00 |
| Medical and dental expenses | $ |
| Transportation | $ 40.00 |
| Recreation, clubs and entertainment, newspapers, magazines, etc. | $ 100.00 |
| Charitable contributions | $ |
| Insurance: (not deducted from wages or included in home mortgage payments) | |
|         Homeowner's or renter's | $ |
|         Life | $ |
|         Health | $ 200.00 |
|         Auto | $ 133.00 |
|         Other _____ | $ |
| Taxes (not deducted from wages or included in home mortgage payments) | |
| (Specify) _____ | $ |
| Installment payments: (In chapter 12 and 13 cases, do not list payments to be included in the plan) | |
|         Auto | $ 209.00 |
|         Other _____ | $ |
|         Other _____ | $ |
| Alimony, maintenance, and support paid to others | $ |
| Payments for support of additional dependents not living at your home | $ |
| Regular expenses from operation of business, profession, or farm (attach detailed statement) | $ |
| Other _____ | $ |

**TOTAL MONTHLY EXPENSES (Report also on Summary of Schedules)**     $ 1,962.00

(FOR CHAPTER 12 AND 13 DEBTORS ONLY)

Provide the information requested below, including whether plan payments are to be made bi-weekly, monthly, annually, or at some other regular interval.

| | |
|---|---:|
| A.  Total projected monthly income | $ |
| B.  Total projected monthly expenses | $ |
| C.  Excess income (A minus B) | $ |
| D.  Total amount to be paid into plan each _____ | $ |
|                            (interval) | |

[BOF6J] SCHEDULE J - CURRENT EXPENDITURES OF INDIVIDUAL DEBTOR(S)

## FORM B6J: SCHEDULE J—CURRENT
## EXPENDITURES OF INDIVIDUAL DEBTOR(S)

IN RE <u>Deborah D. Debtor</u>             Case No. _____
<sub>Debtor(s)</sub>

## DECLARATION CONCERNING DEBTOR'S SCHEDULES

### DECLARATION UNDER PENALTY OF PERJURY BY INDIVIDUAL DEBTOR

I declare under penalty of perjury that I have read the foregoing summary and schedules, consisting of ____16____

<sub>(Total shown on summary page plus 1)</sub>

sheets, and that they are true and correct to the best of my knowledge, information, and belief.

Date: ___11/25/2002___     Signature: _____

                        Deborah D. Debtor

<sub>Debtor</sub>

Date: _____     Signature: _____

<sub>(Joint Debtor, if any)</sub>

[If joint case, both spouses must sign.]

### CERTIFICATION OF NON-ATTORNEY BANKRUPTCY PETITION PREPARER (See 11 U.S.C. § 110)

I certify that I am a bankruptcy petition preparer as defined in 11 U.S.C. § 110, that I prepared this document for compensation, and that I have provided the debtor with a copy of this document.

_____       _____
<sub>Printed or Typed Name of Bankruptcy Petition Preparer</sub>            <sub>Social Security No.</sub>

_____

<sub>Address</sub>

Names and Social Security numbers of all other individuals who prepared or assisted in preparing this document:

If more than one person prepared this document, attach additional signed sheets conforming to the appropriate Official Form for each person.

_____       _____
<sub>Signature of Bankruptcy Petition Preparer</sub>            <sub>Date</sub>

<sub>A bankruptcy petition preparer's failure to comply with the provision of title 11 and the Federal Rules of Bankruptcy Procedures may result in fines or imprisonment or both. 11 U.S.C. § 110; 18 U.S.C. § 156.</sub>

### DECLARATION UNDER PENALTY OF PERJURY ON BEHALF OF CORPORATION OR PARTNERSHIP

I, the _____ (the president or other

officer or an authorized agent of the corporation or a member or an authorized agent of the partnership) of the _____

_____ (corporation or partnership) named as debtor in this case,

declare under penalty of perjury that I have read the foregoing summary and schedules, consisting of _____

<sub>(Total shown on summary page plus 1)</sub>

sheets, and that they are true and correct to the best of my knowledge, information, and belief.

Date: _____     Signature: _____

                      _____

<sub>(Print or type name of individual signing on behalf of debtor)</sub>

[An individual signing on behalf of a partnership or corporation must indicate position or relationship to debtor.]

<sub>Penalty for making a false statement or concealing property. Fine of up to $500,000 or imprisonment for up to 5 years or both. 18 U.S.C. §§ 152 and 3571.</sub>

<sub>[BOF6_] DECLARATION CONCERNING DEBTOR'S SCHEDULES</sub>           <sub>Copyright 1995 M. Mohr, Inc. [1-800-998-2424]</sub>

## FORM B6J: DECLARATION CONCERNING DEBTOR'S SCHEDULES

Form 7
(9/00)

FORM 7.  STATEMENT OF FINANCIAL AFFAIRS

# UNITED STATES BANKRUPTCY COURT

_____ DISTRICT OF _____

In re: _____,        Case No. _____
　　　　　　　(Name)　　　　　　　　　　　　　　　　　　　(if known)
　　　　　　　　　　　　Debtor

## STATEMENT OF FINANCIAL AFFAIRS

　　　　This statement is to be completed by every debtor.  Spouses filing a joint petition may file a single statement on which the information for both spouses is combined.  If the case is filed under chapter 12 or chapter 13, a married debtor must furnish information for both spouses whether or not a joint petition is filed, unless the spouses are separated and a joint petition is not filed.  An individual debtor engaged in business as a sole proprietor, partner, family farmer, or self-employed professional, should provide the information requested on this statement concerning all such activities as well as the individual's personal affairs.

　　　　Questions 1 - 18 are to be completed by all debtors.  Debtors that are or have been in business, as defined below, also must complete Questions 19 - 25.  **If the answer to an applicable question is "None," mark the box labeled "None."**  If additional space is needed for the answer to any question, use and attach a separate sheet properly identified with the case name, case number (if known), and the number of the question.

*DEFINITIONS*

　　　　*"In business."*  A debtor is "in business" for the purpose of this form if the debtor is a corporation or partnership.  An individual debtor is "in business" for the purpose of this form if the debtor is or has been, within the six years immediately preceding the filing of this bankruptcy case, any of the following: an officer, director, managing executive, or owner of 5 percent or more of the voting or equity securities of a corporation; a partner, other than a limited partner, of a partnership; a sole proprietor or self-employed.

　　　　*"Insider."*  The term "insider" includes but is not limited to: relatives of the debtor; general partners of the debtor and their relatives; corporations of which the debtor is an officer, director, or person in control; officers, directors, and any owner of 5 percent or more of the voting or equity securities of a corporate debtor and their relatives; affiliates of the debtor and insiders of such affiliates; any managing agent of the debtor.  11 U.S.C. § 101.

---

1.　**Income from employment or operation of business**

None
☐
　　　State the gross amount of income the debtor has received from employment, trade, or profession, or from operation of the debtor's business from the beginning of this calendar year to the date this case was commenced.  State also the gross amounts received during the **two years** immediately preceding this calendar year.  (A debtor that maintains, or has maintained, financial records on the basis of a fiscal rather than a calendar year may report fiscal year income.  Identify the beginning and ending dates of the debtor's fiscal year.)  If a joint petition is filed, state income for each spouse separately.  (Married debtors filing under chapter 12 or chapter 13 must state income of both spouses whether or not a joint petition is filed, unless the spouses are separated and a joint petition is not filed.)

　　　　AMOUNT　　　　　　　　　　　　　　　SOURCE (if more than one)

## FORM 7: STATEMENT OF FINANCIAL AFFAIRS

## 2. Income other than from employment or operation of business

None
☐

State the amount of income received by the debtor other than from employment, trade, profession, or operation of the debtor's business during the **two years** immediately preceding the commencement of this case. Give particulars. If a joint petition is filed, state income for each spouse separately. (Married debtors filing under chapter 12 or chapter 13 must state income for each spouse whether or not a joint petition is filed, unless the spouses are separated and a joint petition is not filed.)

AMOUNT                                                                      SOURCE

---

## 3. Payments to creditors

None
☐

a.   List all payments on loans, installment purchases of goods or services, and other debts, aggregating more than $600 to any creditor, made within **90 days** immediately preceding the commencement of this case. (Married debtors filing under chapter 12 or chapter 13 must include payments by either or both spouses whether or not a joint petition is filed, unless the spouses are separated and a joint petition is not filed.)

| NAME AND ADDRESS OF CREDITOR | DATES OF PAYMENTS | AMOUNT PAID | AMOUNT STILL OWING |
|---|---|---|---|

---

None
☐

b.   List all payments made within **one year** immediately preceding the commencement of this case to or for the benefit of creditors who are or were insiders. (Married debtors filing under chapter 12 or chapter 13 must include payments by either or both spouses whether or not a joint petition is filed, unless the spouses are separated and a joint petition is not filed.)

| NAME AND ADDRESS OF CREDITOR AND RELATIONSHIP TO DEBTOR | DATE OF PAYMENT | AMOUNT PAID | AMOUNT STILL OWING |
|---|---|---|---|

---

## 4. Suits and administrative proceedings, executions, garnishments and attachments

None
☐

a.   List all suits and administrative proceedings to which the debtor is or was a party within **one year** immediately preceding the filing of this bankruptcy case. (Married debtors filing under chapter 12 or chapter 13 must include information concerning either or both spouses whether or not a joint petition is filed, unless the spouses are separated and a joint petition is not filed.)

| CAPTION OF SUIT AND CASE NUMBER | NATURE OF PROCEEDING | COURT OR AGENCY AND LOCATION | STATUS OR DISPOSITION |
|---|---|---|---|

None ☐    b.   Describe all property that has been attached, garnished or seized under any legal or equitable process within **one year** immediately preceding the commencement of this case. (Married debtors filing under chapter 12 or chapter 13 must include information concerning property of either or both spouses whether or not a joint petition is filed, unless the spouses are separated and a joint petition is not filed.)

| NAME AND ADDRESS OF PERSON FOR WHOSE BENEFIT PROPERTY WAS SEIZED | DATE OF SEIZURE | DESCRIPTION AND VALUE OF PROPERTY |
| --- | --- | --- |

---

### 5. Repossessions, foreclosures and returns

None ☐   List all property that has been repossessed by a creditor, sold at a foreclosure sale, transferred through a deed in lieu of foreclosure or returned to the seller, within **one year** immediately preceding the commencement of this case. (Married debtors filing under chapter 12 or chapter 13 must include information concerning property of either or both spouses whether or not a joint petition is filed, unless the spouses are separated and a joint petition is not filed.)

| NAME AND ADDRESS OF CREDITOR OR SELLER | DATE OF REPOSSESSION, FORECLOSURE SALE, TRANSFER OR RETURN | DESCRIPTION AND VALUE OF PROPERTY |
| --- | --- | --- |

---

### 6. Assignments and receiverships

None ☐    a.   Describe any assignment of property for the benefit of creditors made within **120 days** immediately preceding the commencement of this case. (Married debtors filing under chapter 12 or chapter 13 must include any assignment by either or both spouses whether or not a joint petition is filed, unless the spouses are separated and a joint petition is not filed.)

| NAME AND ADDRESS OF ASSIGNEE | DATE OF ASSIGNMENT | TERMS OF ASSIGNMENT OR SETTLEMENT |
| --- | --- | --- |

---

None ☐    b.   List all property which has been in the hands of a custodian, receiver, or court-appointed official within **one year** immediately preceding the commencement of this case. (Married debtors filing under chapter 12 or chapter 13 must include information concerning property of either or both spouses whether or not a joint petition is filed, unless the spouses are separated and a joint petition is not filed.)

| NAME AND ADDRESS OF CUSTODIAN | NAME AND LOCATION OF COURT CASE TITLE & NUMBER | DATE OF ORDER | DESCRIPTION AND VALUE OF PROPERTY |
| --- | --- | --- | --- |

### 7. Gifts

None
☐

List all gifts or charitable contributions made within **one year** immediately preceding the commencement of this case except ordinary and usual gifts to family members aggregating less than $200 in value per individual family member and charitable contributions aggregating less than $100 per recipient. (Married debtors filing under chapter 12 or chapter 13 must include gifts or contributions by either or both spouses whether or not a joint petition is filed, unless the spouses are separated and a joint petition is not filed.)

| NAME AND ADDRESS OF PERSON OR ORGANIZATION | RELATIONSHIP TO DEBTOR, IF ANY | DATE OF GIFT | DESCRIPTION AND VALUE OF GIFT |
|---|---|---|---|

### 8. Losses

None
☐

List all losses from fire, theft, other casualty or gambling within **one year** immediately preceding the commencement of this case **or since the commencement of this case.** (Married debtors filing under chapter 12 or chapter 13 must include losses by either or both spouses whether or not a joint petition is filed, unless the spouses are separated and a joint petition is not filed.)

| DESCRIPTION AND VALUE OF PROPERTY | DESCRIPTION OF CIRCUMSTANCES AND, IF LOSS WAS COVERED IN WHOLE OR IN PART BY INSURANCE, GIVE PARTICULARS | DATE OF LOSS |
|---|---|---|

### 9. Payments related to debt counseling or bankruptcy

None
☐

List all payments made or property transferred by or on behalf of the debtor to any persons, including attorneys, for consultation concerning debt consolidation, relief under the bankruptcy law or preparation of a petition in bankruptcy within **one year** immediately preceding the commencement of this case.

| NAME AND ADDRESS OF PAYEE | DATE OF PAYMENT, NAME OF PAYOR IF OTHER THAN DEBTOR | AMOUNT OF MONEY OR DESCRIPTION AND VALUE OF PROPERTY |
|---|---|---|

### 10. Other transfers

None
☐

List all other property, other than property transferred in the ordinary course of the business or financial affairs of the debtor, transferred either absolutely or as security within **one year** immediately preceding the commencement of this case. (Married debtors filing under chapter 12 or chapter 13 must include transfers by either or both spouses whether or not a joint petition is filed, unless the spouses are separated and a joint petition is not filed.)

| NAME AND ADDRESS OF TRANSFEREE, RELATIONSHIP TO DEBTOR | DATE | DESCRIBE PROPERTY TRANSFERRED AND VALUE RECEIVED |
|---|---|---|

#### 11. Closed financial accounts

None
☐

List all financial accounts and instruments held in the name of the debtor or for the benefit of the debtor which were closed, sold, or otherwise transferred within **one year** immediately preceding the commencement of this case. Include checking, savings, or other financial accounts, certificates of deposit, or other instruments; shares and share accounts held in banks, credit unions, pension funds, cooperatives, associations, brokerage houses and other financial institutions. (Married debtors filing under chapter 12 or chapter 13 must include information concerning accounts or instruments held by or for either or both spouses whether or not a joint petition is filed, unless the spouses are separated and a joint petition is not filed.)

| NAME AND ADDRESS OF INSTITUTION | TYPE AND NUMBER OF ACCOUNT AND AMOUNT OF FINAL BALANCE | AMOUNT AND DATE OF SALE OR CLOSING |
|---|---|---|

#### 12. Safe deposit boxes

None
☐

List each safe deposit or other box or depository in which the debtor has or had securities, cash, or other valuables within **one year** immediately preceding the commencement of this case. (Married debtors filing under chapter 12 or chapter 13 must include boxes or depositories of either or both spouses whether or not a joint petition is filed, unless the spouses are separated and a joint petition is not filed.)

| NAME AND ADDRESS OF BANK OR OTHER DEPOSITORY | NAMES AND ADDRESSES OF THOSE WITH ACCESS TO BOX OR DEPOSITORY | DESCRIPTION OF CONTENTS | DATE OF TRANSFER OR SURRENDER, IF ANY |
|---|---|---|---|

#### 13. Setoffs

None
☐

List all setoffs made by any creditor, including a bank, against a debt or deposit of the debtor within **90 days** preceding the commencement of this case. (Married debtors filing under chapter 12 or chapter 13 must include information concerning either or both spouses whether or not a joint petition is filed, unless the spouses are separated and a joint petition is not filed.)

| NAME AND ADDRESS OF CREDITOR | DATE OF SETOFF | AMOUNT OF SETOFF |
|---|---|---|

#### 14. Property held for another person

None
☐

List all property owned by another person that the debtor holds or controls.

| NAME AND ADDRESS OF OWNER | DESCRIPTION AND VALUE OF PROPERTY | LOCATION OF PROPERTY |
|---|---|---|

**15. Prior address of debtor**

None ☐

If the debtor has moved within the **two years** immediately preceding the commencement of this case, list all premises which the debtor occupied during that period and vacated prior to the commencement of this case. If a joint petition is filed, report also any separate address of either spouse.

ADDRESS                 NAME USED            DATES OF OCCUPANCY

**16. Spouses and Former Spouses**

None ☐

If the debtor resides or resided in a community property state, commonwealth, or territory (including Alaska, Arizona, California, Idaho, Louisiana, Nevada, New Mexico, Puerto Rico, Texas, Washington, or Wisconsin) within the **six-year period** immediately preceding the commencement of the case, identify the name of the debtor's spouse and of any former spouse who resides or resided with the debtor in the community property state.

NAME

**17. Environmental Information**.

For the purpose of this question, the following definitions apply:

"Environmental Law" means any federal, state, or local statute or regulation regulating pollution, contamination, releases of hazardous or toxic substances, wastes or material into the air, land, soil, surface water, groundwater, or other medium, including, but not limited to, statutes or regulations regulating the cleanup of these substances, wastes, or material.

"Site" means any location, facility, or property as defined under any Environmental Law, whether or not presently or formerly owned or operated by the debtor, including, but not limited to, disposal sites.

"Hazardous Material" means anything defined as a hazardous waste, hazardous substance, toxic substance, hazardous material, pollutant, or contaminant or similar term under an Environmental Law

None ☐

a. List the name and address of every site for which the debtor has received notice in writing by a governmental unit that it may be liable or potentially liable under or in violation of an Environmental Law. Indicate the governmental unit, the date of the notice, and, if known, the Environmental Law:

SITE NAME        NAME AND ADDRESS     DATE OF    ENVIRONMENTAL
AND ADDRESS     OF GOVERNMENTAL UNIT    NOTICE    LAW

None ☐

b. List the name and address of every site for which the debtor provided notice to a governmental unit of a release of Hazardous Material. Indicate the governmental unit to which the notice was sent and the date of the notice.

SITE NAME        NAME AND ADDRESS     DATE OF    ENVIRONMENTAL

AND ADDRESS    OF GOVERNMENTAL UNIT    NOTICE    LAW

None ☐

c.   List all judicial or administrative proceedings, including settlements or orders, under any Environmental Law with respect to which the debtor is or was a party. Indicate the name and address of the governmental unit that is or was a party to the proceeding, and the docket number.

| NAME AND ADDRESS OF GOVERNMENTAL UNIT | DOCKET NUMBER | STATUS OR DISPOSITION |
|---|---|---|

## 18 . Nature, location and name of business

None ☐

a.   If the debtor is an individual, list the names, addresses, taxpayer identification numbers, nature of the businesses, and beginning and ending dates of all businesses in which the debtor was an officer, director, partner, or managing executive of a corporation, partnership, sole proprietorship, or was a self-employed professional within the **six years** immediately preceding the commencement of this case, or in which the debtor owned 5 percent or more of the voting or equity securities within the **six years** immediately preceding the commencement of this case.

      If the debtor is a partnership, list the names, addresses, taxpayer identification numbers, nature of the businesses, and beginning and ending dates of all businesses in which the debtor was a partner or owned 5 percent or more of the voting or equity securities, within the **six years** immediately preceding the commencement of this case.

      If the debtor is a corporation, list the names, addresses, taxpayer identification numbers, nature of the businesses, and beginning and ending dates of all businesses in which the debtor was a partner or owned 5 percent or more of the voting or equity securities within the **six years** immediately preceding the commencement of this case.

| NAME | TAXPAYER I.D. NUMBER | ADDRESS | NATURE OF BUSINESS | BEGINNING AND ENDING DATES |
|---|---|---|---|---|

None ☐

b.   Identify any business listed in response to subdivision a., above, that is "single asset real estate" as defined in 11 U.S.C. § 101.

| NAME | ADDRESS |
|---|---|

    The following questions are to be completed by every debtor that is a corporation or partnership and by any individual debtor who is or has been, within the **six years** immediately preceding the commencement of this case, any of the following: an officer, director, managing executive, or owner of more than 5 percent of the voting or equity securities of a corporation; a partner, other than a limited partner, of a partnership; a sole proprietor or otherwise self-employed.

    *(An individual or joint debtor should complete this portion of the statement **only** if the debtor is or has been in business, as defined above, within the six years immediately preceding the commencement of this case. A debtor who has not been in business within those six years should go directly to the signature page.)*

### 19. Books, records and financial statements

None ☐
a. List all bookkeepers and accountants who within the **two years** immediately preceding the filing of this bankruptcy case kept or supervised the keeping of books of account and records of the debtor.

NAME AND ADDRESS                                    DATES SERVICES RENDERED

None ☐
b. List all firms or individuals who within the **two years** immediately preceding the filing of this bankruptcy case have audited the books of account and records, or prepared a financial statement of the debtor.

NAME                              ADDRESS                    DATES SERVICES RENDERED

None ☐
c. List all firms or individuals who at the time of the commencement of this case were in possession of the books of account and records of the debtor. If any of the books of account and records are not available, explain.

NAME                                                        ADDRESS

None ☐
d. List all financial institutions, creditors and other parties, including mercantile and trade agencies, to whom a financial statement was issued within the **two years** immediately preceding the commencement of this case by the debtor.

NAME AND ADDRESS                                    DATE ISSUED

### 20. Inventories

None ☐
a. List the dates of the last two inventories taken of your property, the name of the person who supervised the taking of each inventory, and the dollar amount and basis of each inventory.

DATE OF INVENTORY        INVENTORY SUPERVISOR        DOLLAR AMOUNT OF INVENTORY
                                                     (Specify cost, market or other basis)

None ☐
b. List the name and address of the person having possession of the records of each of the two inventories reported in a., above.

DATE OF INVENTORY                          NAME AND ADDRESSES OF CUSTODIAN
                                           OF INVENTORY RECORDS

**21 . Current Partners, Officers, Directors and Shareholders**

None ☐    a.    If the debtor is a partnership, list the nature and percentage of partnership interest of each member of the partnership.

NAME AND ADDRESS      NATURE OF INTEREST      PERCENTAGE OF INTEREST

None ☐    b.    If the debtor is a corporation, list all officers and directors of the corporation, and each stockholder who directly or indirectly owns, controls, or holds 5 percent or more of the voting or equity securities of the corporation.

NAME AND ADDRESS      TITLE      NATURE AND PERCENTAGE OF STOCK OWNERSHIP

**22 . Former partners, officers, directors and shareholders**

None ☐    a.    If the debtor is a partnership, list each member who withdrew from the partnership within **one year** immediately preceding the commencement of this case.

NAME      ADDRESS      DATE OF WITHDRAWAL

None ☐    b.    If the debtor is a corporation, list all officers, or directors whose relationship with the corporation terminated within **one year** immediately preceding the commencement of this case.

NAME AND ADDRESS      TITLE      DATE OF TERMINATION

**23 . Withdrawals from a partnership or distributions by a corporation**

None ☐    If the debtor is a partnership or corporation, list all withdrawals or distributions credited or given to an insider, including compensation in any form, bonuses, loans, stock redemptions, options exercised and any other perquisite during **one year** immediately preceding the commencement of this case.

NAME & ADDRESS OF RECIPIENT, RELATIONSHIP TO DEBTOR      DATE AND PURPOSE OF WITHDRAWAL      AMOUNT OF MONEY OR DESCRIPTION AND VALUE OF PROPERTY

**24. Tax Consolidation Group.**

None
☐

If the debtor is a corporation, list the name and federal taxpayer identification number of the parent corporation of any consolidated group for tax purposes of which the debtor has been a member at any time within the **six-year period** immediately preceding the commencement of the case.

NAME OF PARENT CORPORATION        TAXPAYER IDENTIFICATION NUMBER

---

**25. Pension Funds.**

None
☐

If the debtor is not an individual, list the name and federal taxpayer identification number of any pension fund to which the debtor, as an employer, has been responsible for contributing at any time within the **six-year period** immediately preceding the commencement of the case.

NAME OF PENSION FUND        TAXPAYER IDENTIFICATION NUMBER

---

\* \* \* \* \* \*

*[If completed by an individual or individual and spouse]*

I declare under penalty of perjury that I have read the answers contained in the foregoing statement of financial affairs and any attachments thereto and that they are true and correct.

Date _____ Signature _____
of Debtor

Date _____ Signature _____
of Joint Debtor
(if any)

---

*[If completed on behalf of a partnership or corporation]*

I, declare under penalty of perjury that I have read the answers contained in the foregoing statement of financial affairs and any attachments thereto and that they are true and correct to the best of my knowledge, information and belief.

Date _____ Signature _____

_____
Print Name and Title

[An individual signing on behalf of a partnership or corporation must indicate position or relationship to debtor.]

\_\_\_\_ continuation sheets attached

*Penalty for making a false statement: Fine of up to $500,000 or imprisonment for up to 5 years, or both. 18 U.S.C. § 152 and 3571*

----------------------------------------------------------------------------------------------------------------------------------------

**CERTIFICATION AND SIGNATURE OF NON-ATTORNEY BANKRUPTCY PETITION PREPARER (See 11 U.S.C. § 110)**

I certify that I am a bankruptcy petition preparer as defined in 11 U.S.C. § 110, that I prepared this document for compensation, and that I have provided the debtor with a copy of this document.

_____   _____
Printed or Typed Name of Bankruptcy Petition Preparer          Social Security No.

_____

_____
Address

Names and Social Security numbers of all other individuals who prepared or assisted in preparing this document:

If more than one person prepared this document, attach additional signed sheets conforming to the appropriate Official Form for each person.

X _____   _____
Signature of Bankruptcy Petition Preparer                          Date

*A bankruptcy petition preparer's failure to comply with the provisions of title 11 and the Federal Rules of Bankruptcy Procedure may result in fines or imprisonment or both. 18 U.S.C. § 156.*

United States Bankruptcy Court
Southern District of Florida

IN RE

Deborah D. Debtor
107-20-2694

2056 S.E. 117th Street
Pompano Beach, FL 33308

Case No. _____

DEBTOR(S)    Chapter 7 _____

## CHAPTER 7 INDIVIDUAL DEBTOR'S STATEMENT OF INTENTION

1. I have filed a schedule of assets and liabilities which includes consumer debts secured by property of the estate.
2. I intend to do the following with respect to the property of the estate which secures those consumer debts:

   a. *Property to Be Surrendered.*

   | Description of Property | Creditor's Name |
   |---|---|
   | | |
   | | |
   | | |

   b. *Property to Be Retained.  [Check any applicable statement.]*

   | Description of Property | Creditor's Name | Property is claimed as exempt | Property will be redeemed pursuant to §722 | Debt will be reaffirmed pursuant to §524(c) |
   |---|---|---|---|---|
   | Debtor's American Va-Zoom | American Auto Retailers | | | X |
   | Debtor's Homestead Real Pr | Pompano National Mortgage | | | X |
   | | | | | |
   | | | | | |
   | | | | | |
   | | | | | |

Date: 11/25/2002 _____

Debtor Deborah D. Debtor          Joint Debtor (if any)

### CERTIFICATION OF NON-ATTORNEY BANKRUPTCY PETITION PREPARER (See 11 U.S.C. § 110)

I certify that I am a bankruptcy petition preparer as defined in 11 U.S.C. § 110, that I prepared this document for compensation, and that I have provided the debtor with a copy of this document.

Printed or Typed Name of Bankruptcy Petition Preparer          Social Security No.

Address

Names and Social Security numbers of all other individuals who prepared or assisted in preparing this document:

If more than one person prepared this document, attach additional signed sheets conforming to the appropriate Official Form for each person.

Signature of Bankruptcy Petition Preparer          Date

A bankruptcy petition preparer's failure to comply with the provision of title 11 and the Federal Rules of Bankruptcy Procedures may result in fines or imprisonment or both. 11 U.S.C. § 110; 18 U.S.C. § 156.

[BOF8] CHAPTER 7 INDIVIDUAL DEBTOR'S STATEMENT OF INTENTION          Copyright 1997 M. Mohr, Inc. [1-800-998-2424]

## FORM B8: INDIVIDUAL DEBTOR'S STATEMENT OF INTENTION

**United States Bankruptcy Court**
**Southern District of Florida**

IN RE

Deborah D. Debtor
107-20-2694

2056 S.E. 117th Street                          Case No. _____
Pompano Beach, FL  33308

                                    **DEBTOR(S)**      Chapter _7_____

## VERIFICATION OF CREDITOR MATRIX

The above named debtor hereby verifies that the attached matrix listing creditors is true to the best of my knowledge.

Date: ___11/25/2002___      Signature: _____
                                        Deborah D. Debtor                      Debtor

Date: _____      Signature: _____
                                                              (Joint Debtor, if any)

Date: ___11/25/2002___      Signature: _____
                                                                      Attorney

Copyright 1998 M. Mohr, Inc. [1-800-998-2424]

## VERIFICATION OF CREDITOR MATRIX

Alternative Risk Management
12 Buspar Way
Mt. Rushmore, IL 90766

American Auto Retailers
1000 CarLoan Way
Fort Lauderdale, FL 33305

Cell Phones Unlimited
32 N.W. 132 Street
Fort Lauderdale, FL 33505

Clammy Collector, Esq.
Mr. Clammy Collector
999 Grabbit Way
Miami, FL 33168

Credit Collectors
Ms. Getta Job
123 Paxel Way
Pompano Beach, FL 33099

Discover
P.O. Box 9088
Phoenix, TX 85033-9088

Drs. Helliard & Cuttum
1223 Buzzsaw Lane
Weston, FL 33455

Large Department Store
111 Department Store Way
Westin, FL 33022

MCP Financial Inc.
Ms. Lucy Head
400 Slimegrub Blvd.
Pittsburgh, PA 06666

Med Collectors, Inc.
Ms. Madi Collector
100 Sludgebuckets Road
Pittsburgh, PA 09988

Pompano National Mortgage
112 North Atlantic Ave.
Pompano, FL 33211

Sears Premier Card
Payment Center Annex
86 Annex
Eastridge, GA 30789-0001

Whalersville Emergency Phys
966 Bottomfeeders Way
Whalersville, FL 33089

Whalersville Hospital
999 Bottomfeeders Way
Whalersville, FL 33456

# Federal and State Personal Bankruptcy Exemptions

All states have exemptions for certain property and for the homestead. These exemptions are important in preplanning your bankruptcy and in understanding the possible outcome of your decisions. Each state is different and has a certain autonomy in determining the exemptions available for its citizens. Many states allow the debtor to choose between the federal and state exemption allowances according to what will be most beneficial. On the other hand, many states require that only the state exemptions be allowed.

State exemptions vary. The idea is to give you the opportunity to meet your obligations while being able to get back on your feet. These exemptions represent what you can keep in the event of a liquidation bankruptcy. This exempt property does not become part of the trustee's estate.

Following are the federal exemptions as they exist now before any reform.

## FEDERAL EXEMPTIONS

According to:

Title 11 U.S.C. Section 522

Married couples double the amount of the following federal exemptions:

- Homestead—Real property, including co-op or mobile home, to $17,450; unused portion of homestead to $8,725 may be applied to any property.

- Life insurance payments for person you depended on, needed for support.

- Life insurance policy with loan value, in accrued dividends or interest to $9,300.

- Unmatured life insurance contract, except credit insurance policy.

- Alimony, child support needed for support.

- Pensions and Retirement Benefits—ERISA—qualified benefits needed for support.

- Household goods and furnishings $9,300 total.

- Health Aids.

- Jewelry to $1,150.

- Lost earnings payments.

- Motor vehicle to $2,775.

- Personal injury compensation payments to $17,425.

- Wrongful death payments.

- Crime victims' compensation.

- Public assistance.

- Social Security.

- Unemployment compensation.

- Veterans' benefits.

- Tools of trade—books and equipment to $1,750.

- Wild Card—$925 of any property plus up to $8,725 of any amount of unused homestead exemption.

Here are the individual states that do not give the debtors the option of electing either the federal or state exemptions. In the following states, only the state exemption standards apply. Take note of whether or not your state allows you to choose and be sure to research your particular state carefully as we only provide you with preliminary information. There is a very comprehensive Web site devoted to information about bankruptcy and in particular, any updated information about exemptions. On this site—http://www .BankruptcyAction.com—you can find telephone numbers and detailed explanations of your state's peculiarities. This site is a highly valuable resource. They can be contacted by e-mail with the address webmaster//www.insol.org). This organization published a "Consumer Debt Report" in May of 2001 that can be found on their site that provides valuable information about this issue as well as information regarding how the new reform will influence exemptions and bankruptcy planning.

The following is a list of states that permit only the use of their individual state's exemptions:

- Alabama
- Alaska
- Arizona
- California
- Colorado
- Delaware
- Florida
- Georgia
- Idaho
- Illinois
- Indiana
- Iowa
- Kansas
- Louisiana
- Maine
- Maryland
- Missouri
- Montana
- Nebraska
- Nevada
- New Hampshire
- New York
- North Carolina
- North Dakota
- Ohio
- Oklahoma
- Oregon
- South Carolina
- South Dakota
- Tennessee
- Utah
- Vermont
- Virginia
- West Virginia
- Wyoming

The following states allow the debtor to choose between the state exemptions or the federal exemptions depending upon which would be most advantageous under the particular facts of the case:

- Arkansas
- Connecticut
- Hawaii
- Massachusetts
- Michigan
- Minnesota
- Mississippi
- New Jersey

- New Mexico
- Pennsylvania
- Puerto Rico

- Rhode Island
- District of Columbia
- Wisconsin

$17,450 is the amount of the homestead exemption under the federal standard. This represents the amount of equity in your house you will be able to keep or use otherwise in the preparation of your case. Under the federal standard this is doubled for married couples. In the states that permit only the state standard to be used, the homestead exemptions vary tremendously. For example:

- The Alabama statutes permit exemption of a debtor's homestead up to the amount of $5,000.00 (C.O.A. 6–10-2).

- In Alaska, an individual is entitled to a homestead exemption of the individual's interest in property in the State of Alaska used as the principal residence of the individual or the dependents of the individual, but the value of the homestead exemption may not exceed $64,800 (Section 09.38.010(a)).

- In Arizona, the exemption amount is from attachment, execution and forced sale, is up to but not exceeding one hundred thousand dollars in value ($100,000). Only one homestead exemption may be held by a married couple or a single person under the provisions of Arizona law (ARS 33–1101, et seq.).

- Under the Utah Exemption Act (Utah Code 78–23-1 et seq.), a person's homestead is exempt up to $20,000 in value (Utah Code 78–23-3(d)). A homestead may consist of a dwelling or mobile home and the land surrounding it, not exceeding one acre, which is being used as his primary personal residence. The amount of homestead exemption an individual may claim cannot exceed $20,000 in value. If the property claimed as exempt is jointly owned, each joint owner is entitled to a homestead exemption but the maximum exemption may not exceed $40,000 (Utah Code 78–23-3(1)).

As you can see, there is quite a variation from state to state.

Other forms of personal property will vary as well. In North Dakota, you can exempt a motor vehicle up to $1,200. In North Carolina, it is $1500. Montana allows one motor vehicle not to exceed $2,500 in value, and while Florida is said to be a debtor's haven for homestead exemptions, it only allows a motor vehicle exemption up to a value of $1,000.

There are many other specific items of personal property whose exemptions vary widely from state to state. Be sure to check your state's specifics when preparing your paperwork. Otherwise consult a lawyer who can help you maximize the outcome of your bankruptcy filing.

It is not going to be fun to give up any of your belongings, but rest assured that each state has allowances for personal items such as photo albums and sentimental items. While they may be priceless to you, they have very little value to a bankruptcy trustee.

# Appendix D

# The Fair Debt Collection Practices Act

We have included the text of the Fair Debt Collection Practices Act so you can see the extent of your rights. Your goal is to get a fresh start by taking care of debts that you can handle and by seeking relief either through proper counseling or if necessary, bankruptcy. You do not have to be harassed or humiliated or condemned or bullied. The law is here to protect you from abusive practices from creditors whose only goal is to collect. The laws are designed to make debt collection reasonable while eliminating the "shake down" methods of intimidation. These are your rights. This document supports our contention that there is support for consumer and debtor protection. You are not a pariah. You are in the process of straightening out your financial life. We all make mistakes. There is help available for you.

*As amended by Public Law 104–208, 110 Stat. 3009 (Sept. 30, 1996)*

*To amend the Consumer Credit Protection Act to prohibit abusive practices by debt collectors.*

Be it enacted by the Senate and House of Representatives of the United States of America in Congress assembled, *That the Consumer Credit Protection Act (15 U.S.C. 1601 et seq.) is amended by adding at the end thereof the following new title:*

## III—DEBT COLLECTION PRACTICES
### (Fair Debt Collection Practices Act)

## § 801. SHORT TITLE (15 USC 1601 NOTE)

This title may be cited as the "Fair Debt Collection Practices Act."

## § 802. CONGRESSIONAL FINDINGS AND DECLARATIONS OF PURPOSE (15 USC 1692)

(a) There is abundant evidence of the use of abusive, deceptive, and unfair debt collection practices by many debt collectors. Abusive debt collection practices contribute to the number of personal bankruptcies, to marital instability, to the loss of jobs, and to invasions of individual privacy.

(b) Existing laws and procedures for redressing these injuries are inadequate to protect consumers.

(c) Means other than misrepresentation or other abusive debt collection practices are available for the effective collection of debts.

(d) Abusive debt collection practices are carried on to a substantial extent in interstate commerce and through means and instrumentalities of such commerce. Even where abusive debt collection practices are purely intrastate in character, they nevertheless directly affect interstate commerce.

(e) It is the purpose of this title to eliminate abusive debt collection practices by debt collectors, to insure that those debt collectors who refrain from using abusive debt collection practices are not competitively disadvantaged, and to promote consistent State action to protect consumers against debt collection abuses.

## § 803. DEFINITIONS [15 USC 1692A]

As used in this title—

(1) The term "Commission" means the Federal Trade Commission.

(2) The term "communication" means the conveying of information regarding a debt directly or indirectly to any person through any medium.

(3) The term "consumer" means any natural person obligated or allegedly obligated to pay any debt.

(4) The term "creditor" means any person who offers or extends credit creating a debt or to whom a debt is owed, but such term does not include any person to the extent that he receives an assignment or transfer of a debt in default solely for the purpose of facilitating collection of such debt for another.

(5) The term "debt" means any obligation or alleged obligation of a consumer to pay money arising out of a transaction in which the money, property, insurance or services which are the subject of the transaction are primarily for personal, family, or household purposes, whether or not such obligation has been reduced to judgment.

(6) The term "debt collector" means any person who uses any instrumentality of interstate commerce or the mails in any business the principal purpose of which is the collection of any debts, or who regularly collects or attempts to collect, directly or indirectly, debts owed or due or asserted to be owed or due another. Notwithstanding the exclusion provided by clause (F) of the last sentence of this

paragraph, the term includes any creditor who, in the process of collecting his own debts, uses any name other than his own which would indicate that a third person is collecting or attempting to collect such debts. For the purpose of section 808(6), such term also includes any person who uses any instrumentality of interstate commerce or the mails in any business the principal purpose of which is the enforcement of security interests. The term does not include—

(A) any officer or employee of a creditor while, in the name of the creditor, collecting debts for such creditor;

(B) any person while acting as a debt collector for another person, both of whom are related by common ownership or affiliated by corporate control, if the person acting as a debt collector does so only for persons to whom it is so related or affiliated and if the principal business of such person is not the collection of debts;

(C) any officer or employee of the United States or any State to the extent that collecting or attempting to collect any debt is in the performance of his official duties;

(D) any person while serving or attempting to serve legal process on any other person in connection with the judicial enforcement of any debt;

(E) any nonprofit organization which, at the request of consumers, performs bona fide consumer credit counseling and assists consumers in the liquidation of their debts by receiving payments from such consumers and distributing such amounts to creditors; and

(F) any person collecting or attempting to collect any debt owed or due or asserted to be owed or due another to the extent such activity (i) is incidental to a bona fide fiduciary obligation or a bona fide escrow arrangement; (ii) concerns a debt which was originated by such person; (iii) concerns a debt which was not in default at the time it was obtained by such person; or (iv) concerns a debt obtained by such person as a secured party in a commercial credit transaction involving the creditor.

(7) The term "location information" means a consumer's place of abode and his telephone number at such place, or his place of employment.

(8) The term "State" means any State, territory, or possession of the United States, the District of Columbia, the Commonwealth of Puerto Rico, or any political subdivision of any of the foregoing.

## § 804. ACQUISITION OF LOCATION INFORMATION [15 USC 1692B]

Any debt collector communicating with any person other than the consumer for the purpose of acquiring location information about the consumer shall—

(1) identify himself, state that he is confirming or correcting location information concerning the consumer, and, only if expressly requested, identify his employer;

(2) not state that such consumer owes any debt;

(3) not communicate with any such person more than once unless requested to do so by such person or unless the debt collector reasonably believes that the earlier response of such person is erroneous or incomplete and that such person now has correct or complete location information;

(4) not communicate by postcard;

(5) not use any language or symbol on any envelope or in the contents of any communication effected by the mails or telegram that indicates that the debt collector is in the debt collection business or that the communication relates to the collection of a debt; and

(6) after the debt collector knows the consumer is represented by an attorney with regard to the subject debt and has knowledge of, or can readily ascertain, such attorney's name and address, not communicate with any person other than that attorney, unless the attorney fails to respond within a reasonable period of time to the communication from the debt collector.

## § 805. COMMUNICATION IN CONNECTION WITH DEBT COLLECTION [15 USC 1692C]

(a) COMMUNICATION WITH THE CONSUMER GENERALLY. Without the prior consent of the consumer given directly to the debt collector or the express permission of a court of competent jurisdiction, a debt collector may not communicate with a consumer in connection with the collection of any debt—

(1) at any unusual time or place or a time or place known or which should be known to be inconvenient to the consumer. In the absence of knowledge of circumstances to the contrary, a debt collector shall assume that the convenient time for communicating with a consumer is after 8 o'clock antimeridian and before 9 o'clock postmeridian, local time at the consumer's location;

(2) if the debt collector knows the consumer is represented by an attorney with respect to such debt and has knowledge of, or can readily ascertain, such attorney's name and address, unless the attorney fails to respond within a reasonable period of time to a communication from the debt collector or unless the attorney consents to direct communication with the consumer; or

(3) at the consumer's place of employment if the debt collector knows or has reason to know that the consumer's employer prohibits the consumer from receiving such communication.

(b) COMMUNICATION WITH THIRD PARTIES. Except as provided in section 804, without the prior consent of the consumer given directly to the debt collector, or the express permission of a court of competent jurisdiction, or as reasonably necessary to effectuate a postjudgment judicial remedy, a debt collector may not communicate, in connection with the collection of any debt, with any person other than a consumer, his attorney, a consumer reporting agency if otherwise permitted by law, the creditor, the attorney of the creditor, or the attorney of the debt collector.

(c) CEASING COMMUNICATION. If a consumer notifies a debt collector in writing that the consumer refuses to pay a debt or that the consumer wishes the debt collector to cease further communication with the consumer, the debt collector shall not communicate further with the consumer with respect to such debt, except—

(1) to advise the consumer that the debt collector's further efforts are being terminated;

(2) to notify the consumer that the debt collector or creditor may invoke specified remedies which are ordinarily invoked by such debt collector or creditor; or

(3) where applicable, to notify the consumer that the debt collector or creditor intends to invoke a specified remedy.

If such notice from the consumer is made by mail, notification shall be complete upon receipt.

(d) For the purpose of this section, the term "consumer" includes the consumer's spouse, parent (if the consumer is a minor), guardian, executor, or administrator.

## § 806. HARASSMENT OR ABUSE [15 USC 1692D]

A debt collector may not engage in any conduct the natural consequence of which is to harass, oppress, or abuse any person in connection with the collection of a debt. Without limiting the general application of the foregoing, the following conduct is a violation of this section:

(1) The use or threat of use of violence or other criminal means to harm the physical person, reputation, or property of any person.

(2) The use of obscene or profane language or language the natural consequence of which is to abuse the hearer or reader.

(3) The publication of a list of consumers who allegedly refuse to pay debts, except to a consumer reporting agency or to persons meeting the requirements of section 603(f) or 604(3)1 of this Act.

(4) The advertisement for sale of any debt to coerce payment of the debt.

(5) Causing a telephone to ring or engaging any person in telephone conversation repeatedly or continuously with intent to annoy, abuse, or harass any person at the called number.

(6) Except as provided in section 804, the placement of telephone calls without meaningful disclosure of the caller's identity.

## § 807. FALSE OR MISLEADING REPRESENTATIONS [15 USC 1962E]

A debt collector may not use any false, deceptive, or misleading representation or means in connection with the collection of any debt. Without limiting the general application of the foregoing, the following conduct is a violation of this section:

(1) The false representation or implication that the debt collector is vouched for, bonded by, or affiliated with the United States or any State, including the use of any badge, uniform, or facsimile thereof.

(2) The false representation of—

(A) the character, amount, or legal status of any debt; or

(B) any services rendered or compensation which may be lawfully received by any debt collector for the collection of a debt.

(3) The false representation or implication that any individual is an attorney or that any communication is from an attorney.

(4) The representation or implication that nonpayment of any debt will result in the arrest or imprisonment of any person or the seizure, garnishment, attachment, or sale of any property or wages of any person unless such action is lawful and the debt collector or creditor intends to take such action.

(5) The threat to take any action that cannot legally be taken or that is not intended to be taken.

(6) The false representation or implication that a sale, referral, or other transfer of any interest in a debt shall cause the consumer to—

(A) lose any claim or defense to payment of the debt; or

(B) become subject to any practice prohibited by this title.

(7) The false representation or implication that the consumer committed any crime or other conduct in order to disgrace the consumer.

(8) Communicating or threatening to communicate to any person credit information which is known or which should be known to be false, including the failure to communicate that a disputed debt is disputed.

(9) The use or distribution of any written communication which simulates or is falsely represented to be a document authorized, issued, or approved by any court, official, or agency of the United States or any State, or which creates a false impression as to its source, authorization, or approval.

(10) The use of any false representation or deceptive means to collect or attempt to collect any debt or to obtain information concerning a consumer.

(11) The failure to disclose in the initial written communication with the consumer and, in addition, if the initial communication with the consumer is oral, in that initial oral communication, that the debt collector is attempting to collect a debt and that any information obtained will be used for that purpose, and the failure to disclose in subsequent communications that the communication is from a debt collector, except that this paragraph shall not apply to a formal pleading made in connection with a legal action.

(12) The false representation or implication that accounts have been turned over to innocent purchasers for value.

(13) The false representation or implication that documents are legal process.

(14) The use of any business, company, or organization name other than the true name of the debt collector's business, company, or organization.

(15) The false representation or implication that documents are not legal process forms or do not require action by the consumer.

(16) The false representation or implication that a debt collector operates or is employed by a consumer reporting agency as defined by section 603(f) of this Act.

## § 808. UNFAIR PRACTICES [15 USC 1692F]

A debt collector may not use unfair or unconscionable means to collect or attempt to collect any debt. Without limiting the general application of the foregoing, the following conduct is a violation of this section:

(1) The collection of any amount (including any interest, fee, charge, or expense incidental to the principal obligation) unless such amount is expressly authorized by the agreement creating the debt or permitted by law.

(2) The acceptance by a debt collector from any person of a check or other payment instrument postdated by more than five days unless such person is notified in writing of the debt collector's intent to deposit such check or instrument not more than ten nor less than three business days prior to such deposit.

(3) The solicitation by a debt collector of any postdated check or other postdated payment instrument for the purpose of threatening or instituting criminal prosecution.

(4) Depositing or threatening to deposit any postdated check or other postdated payment instrument prior to the date on such check or instrument.

(5) Causing charges to be made to any person for communications by concealment of the true propose of the communication. Such charges include, but are not limited to, collect telephone calls and telegram fees.

(6) Taking or threatening to take any nonjudicial action to effect dispossession or disablement of property if—

(A) there is no present right to possession of the property claimed as collateral through an enforceable security interest;

(B) there is no present intention to take possession of the property; or

(C) the property is exempt by law from such dispossession or disablement.

(7) Communicating with a consumer regarding a debt by postcard.

(8) Using any language or symbol, other than the debt collector's address, on any envelope when communicating with a consumer by use of the mails or by telegram, except that a debt collector may use his business name if such name does not indicate that he is in the debt collection business.

## § 809. VALIDATION OF DEBTS [15 USC 1692G]

(a) Within five days after the initial communication with a consumer in connection with the collection of any debt, a debt collector shall, unless the following information is contained in the initial communication or the consumer has paid the debt, send the consumer a written notice containing—

(1) the amount of the debt;

(2) the name of the creditor to whom the debt is owed;

(3) a statement that unless the consumer, within thirty days after receipt of the notice, disputes the validity of the debt, or any portion thereof, the debt will be assumed to be valid by the debt collector;

(4) a statement that if the consumer notifies the debt collector in writing within the thirty-day period that the debt, or any portion thereof, is disputed, the debt collector will obtain verification of the debt or a copy of a judgment against the consumer and a copy of such verification or judgment will be mailed to the consumer by the debt collector; and

(5) a statement that, upon the consumer's written request within the thirty-day period, the debt collector will provide the consumer with the name and address of the original creditor, if different from the current creditor.

(b) If the consumer notifies the debt collector in writing within the thirty-day period described in subsection (a) that the debt, or any portion thereof, is disputed, or that the consumer requests the name and address of the original creditor, the debt collector shall cease collection of the debt, or any disputed portion thereof, until the debt collector obtains verification of the debt or any copy of a judgment, or the name and address of the original creditor, and a copy of such verification or judgment, or name and address of the original creditor, is mailed to the consumer by the debt collector.

(c) The failure of a consumer to dispute the validity of a debt under this section may not be construed by any court as an admission of liability by the consumer.

## § 810. MULTIPLE DEBTS [15 USC 1692H]

If any consumer owes multiple debts and makes any single payment to any debt collector with respect to such debts, such debt collector may not apply such payment to any debt which is disputed by the consumer and, where applicable, shall apply such payment in accordance with the consumer's directions.

## § 811. LEGAL ACTIONS BY DEBT COLLECTORS [15 USC 1692I]

(a) Any debt collector who brings any legal action on a debt against any consumer shall—

(1) in the case of an action to enforce an interest in real property securing the consumer's obligation, bring such action only in a judicial district or similar legal entity in which such real property is located; or

(2) in the case of an action not described in paragraph (1), bring such action only in the judicial district or similar legal entity—

(A) in which such consumer signed the contract sued upon; or

(B) in which such consumer resides at the commencement of the action.

(b) Nothing in this title shall be construed to authorize the bringing of legal actions by debt collectors.

## § 812. FURNISHING CERTAIN DECEPTIVE FORMS [15 USC 1692J]

(a) It is unlawful to design, compile, and furnish any form knowing that such form would be used to create the false belief in a consumer that a person other than the creditor of such consumer is participating in the collection of or in an attempt to collect a debt such consumer allegedly owes such creditor, when in fact such person is not so participating.

(b) Any person who violates this section shall be liable to the same extent and in the same manner as a debt collector is liable under section 813 for failure to comply with a provision of this title.

## § 813. CIVIL LIABILITY [15 USC 1692K]

(a) Except as otherwise provided by this section, any debt collector who fails to comply with any provision of this title with respect to any person is liable to such person in an amount equal to the sum of—

(1) any actual damage sustained by such person as a result of such failure;

(2) (A) in the case of any action by an individual, such additional damages as the court may allow, but not exceeding $1,000; or

(B) in the case of a class action, (i) such amount for each named plaintiff as could be recovered under subparagraph (A), and (ii) such amount as the court may allow for all other class members, without regard to a minimum individual recovery, not to exceed the lesser of $500,000 or 1 per centum of the net worth of the debt collector; and

(3) in the case of any successful action to enforce the foregoing liability, the costs of the action, together with a reasonable attorney's fee as determined by the court. On a finding by the court that an action under this section was brought in bad faith and for the purpose of harassment, the court may award to the defendant attorney's fees reasonable in relation to the work expended and costs.

(b) In determining the amount of liability in any action under subsection (a), the court shall consider, among other relevant factors—

(1) in any individual action under subsection (a)(2)(A), the frequency and persistence of noncompliance by the debt collector, the nature of such noncompliance, and the extent to which such noncompliance was intentional; or

(2) in any class action under subsection (a)(2)(B), the frequency and persistence of noncompliance by the debt collector, the nature of such noncompliance, the resources of the debt collector, the number of persons adversely affected, and the extent to which the debt collector's noncompliance was intentional.

(c) A debt collector may not be held liable in any action brought under this title if the debt collector shows by a preponderance of evidence that the violation was not intentional and resulted from a bona fide error notwithstanding the maintenance of procedures reasonably adapted to avoid any such error.

(d) An action to enforce any liability created by this title may be brought in any appropriate United States district court without regard to the amount in controversy, or in any other court of competent jurisdiction, within one year from the date on which the violation occurs.

(e) No provision of this section imposing any liability shall apply to any act done or omitted in good faith in conformity with any advisory opinion of the Commission, notwithstanding that after such act or omission has occurred, such opinion is amended, rescinded, or determined by judicial or other authority to be invalid for any reason.

## § 814. ADMINISTRATIVE ENFORCEMENT [15 USC 1692L]

(a) Compliance with this title shall be enforced by the Commission, except to the extend that enforcement of the requirements imposed under this title is specifically committed to another agency under subsection (b). For purpose of the exercise by the Commission of its functions and powers under the Federal Trade Commission Act, a violation of this title shall be deemed an unfair or deceptive act or practice in violation of that Act. All of the functions and powers of the Commission under the Federal Trade Commission Act are available to the Commission to enforce compliance by any person with this title, irrespective of whether that person is engaged in commerce or meets any other jurisdictional tests in the Federal Trade Commission Act, including the power to enforce the provisions of this title in the same manner as if the violation had been a violation of a Federal Trade Commission trade regulation rule.

(b) Compliance with any requirements imposed under this title shall be enforced under—

(1) section 8 of the Federal Deposit Insurance Act, in the case of—

(A) national banks, by the Comptroller of the Currency;

(B) member banks of the Federal Reserve System (other than national banks), by the Federal Reserve Board; and

(C) banks the deposits or accounts of which are insured by the Federal Deposit Insurance Corporation (other than members of the Federal Reserve System), by the Board of Directors of the Federal Deposit Insurance Corporation;

(2) section 5(d) of the Home Owners Loan Act of 1933, section 407 of the National Housing Act, and sections 6(i) and 17 of the Federal Home Loan Bank Act, by the Federal Home Loan Bank Board (acting directing or through the Federal Savings and Loan Insurance Corporation), in the case of any institution subject to any of those provisions;

(3) the Federal Credit Union Act, by the Administrator of the National Credit Union Administration with respect to any Federal credit union;

(4) subtitle IV of Title 49, by the Interstate Commerce Commission with respect to any common carrier subject to such subtitle;

(5) the Federal Aviation Act of 1958, by the Secretary of Transportation with respect to any air carrier or any foreign air carrier subject to that Act; and

(6) the Packers and Stockyards Act, 1921 (except as provided in section 406 of that Act), by the Secretary of Agriculture with respect to any activities subject to that Act.

(c) For the purpose of the exercise by any agency referred to in subsection (b) of its powers under any Act referred to in that subsection, a violation of any requirement imposed under this title shall be deemed to be a violation of a requirement imposed under that Act. In addition to its powers under any provision of law specifically referred to in subsection (b), each of the agencies referred to in that subsection may exercise, for the purpose of enforcing compliance with any requirement imposed under this title any other authority conferred on it by law, except as provided in subsection (d).

(d) Neither the Commission nor any other agency referred to in subsection (b) may promulgate trade regulation rules or other regulations with respect to the collection of debts by debt collectors as defined in this title.

## § 815. REPORTS TO CONGRESS BY THE COMMISSION [15 USC 1692M]

(a) Not later than one year after the effective date of this title and at one-year intervals thereafter, the Commission shall make reports to the Congress concerning the administration of its functions under this title, including such recommendations as the Commission deems necessary or appropriate. In addition, each report of the Commission shall include its assessment of the extent to which compliance with this title is being achieved and a summary of the enforcement actions taken by the Commission under section 814 of this title.

(b) In the exercise of its functions under this title, the Commission may obtain upon request the views of any other Federal agency which exercises enforcement functions under section 814 of this title.

## § 816. RELATION TO STATE LAWS [15 USC 1692N]

This title does not annul, alter, or affect, or exempt any person subject to the provisions of this title from complying with the laws of any State with respect to debt collection practices, except to the extent that those laws are inconsistent with any provision of this title, and then only to the extent of the inconsistency. For purposes of this section, a State law is not inconsistent with this title if the protection such law affords any consumer is greater than the protection provided by this title.

## § 817. EXEMPTION FOR STATE REGULATION [15 USC 1692O]

The Commission shall by regulation exempt from the requirements of this title any class of debt collection practices within any State if the Commission determines that under the law of that State that class of debt collection practices is subject to requirements substantially similar to those imposed by this title, and that there is adequate provision for enforcement.

## § 818. EFFECTIVE DATE [15 USC 1692 NOTE]

This title takes effect upon the expiration of six months after the date of its enactment, but section 809 shall apply only with respect to debts for which the initial attempt to collect occurs after such effective date.

Approved September 20, 1977

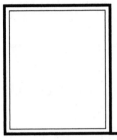

# Bibliography

There are many books and Web sites on bankruptcy, credit, and credit repair. Here are some resources that might be useful as you explore the path of money savvy and fresh-start freedom.

**Books**

*Bankruptcy: Is It the Right Solution to Your Debt Problems? (Quick and Legal Series),* by Robin Leonard and L. M. Lawson (Santa Cruz, CA: Nolo Press, 2002).

*Become Totally Debt Free in Five Years or Less,* by Gwendolyn D. Gabriel, Raphael Elizalde, Chandra Sparks Taylor, and Diana Kennedy (Hastings, MI: Brown Bag, 2000).

*Bounce Back from Bankruptcy: A Step-by-Step Guide to Getting Back on Your Financial Feet* (3rd ed.), by Paula Langguth Ryan (Odenton, MD: Pellingham Casper Communications, 2001).

*The Budget Kit: The Common Cents Money Management Workbook* (3rd ed.) by Judy Lawrence (Chicago: Dearborn Trade, 2000).

*Budget Yes! 21st Century Solutions for Taking Control of Your Money Now!,* by John L. Macko and Jane E. Chidester (Vermilion, OH: Tulip Tree PR, 1998).

*Credit After Bankruptcy: A Step-by-Step Action Plan to Quick and Lasting Recovery after Personal Bankruptcy* (reprint ed.), by Stephen Snyder (McDonough, GA: Bellwether, 2000).

*Credit Card & Debt Management: A Step-By-Step How-To Guide for Organizing Debt & Saving Money on Interest Payments,* by Scott Bilker (Barnegat, NJ: Press One, 1996).

*Credit Card Debt: Reduce Your Financial Burden in Three Easy Steps,* by Alexander Daskaloff (New York: Avon, 1999).

*Currency of Hope,* by Debtors Anonymous (Needham, MA: General Service Board of Trustees (1999).

*Debt Free!: Your Guide to Personal Bankruptcy Without Shame,* by James P. Caher and John M. Caher (New York: Henry Holt 1996).

*The Debtor's Guide to Dumping Collection Agencies,* by B. R. Gordon (Los Angeles: Twintwo Communications, 1997).

*The Guerrilla Guide to Credit Repair: How to Find Out What's Wrong With Your Credit Rating-And How to Fix It,* by Todd Bierman and Nathaniel Wice (New York: St. Martin's Press, 1994).

*How to Get Out of Debt, Stay Out of Debt & Live Prosperously,* by Jerrold J. Mundis (New York: Bantam Doubleday Dell, 2003).

*Mary Hunt's Debt Proof Living,* by Mary Hunt (Nashville, TN: Broadman & Holman, 1999).

*Money Drunk, Money Sober, 90 Days to Financial Freedom,* by Mark Bryan and Julia Cameron (New York: Ballantine Books, 1999).

*Out of Debt: How to Clean Up Your Credit and Balance Your Budget While Avoiding Bankruptcy,* by Robert Steinback (Avon, MA: Adams Media Corporation, 1989).

*The Pocket Idiot's Guide to Living on a Budget,* by Peter J. Sander and Jennifer Basye Sander (Church, CA: Alpha Books, 1999).

*The Unofficial Guide to Beating Debt,* by Greg Pahl (New York: Wiley, 2000).

*Your Rights When You Owe Too Much,* by Gudrun M. Nickel and Brette McWhorter Sember (Basel, Switzerland: Sphinx, 2001).

## Web Sites

American Bankrupty Institute
www.abiworld.org

American Consumer Credit Counseling
www.consumercredit.com
800-769-3571

American Credit Counselors
www.americancredit.org/index.asp?RCID=13
866-260-5994

Christian Financial Ministries
www.good-steward.org/sure.html

Consolidated Credit Counseling Services
www.debtfree.org
800-728-3632, Fax: 866-236-0103

Consumer Credit Counseling Center
www.thedebtprofessional.com/consumer_credit_counseling
_center.htm

National Association of Consumer Bankruptcy Attorneys
nacba.com

National Foundation for Credit Counseling
www.nfcc.org and www.debtadvice.org
800-388-2227 for 24-hour automated office listings

Visual Credit Counseling
www.visual-credit-counseling.org
877-606-6144

**Official U.S. Bankruptcy Forms**

www.uscourts.gov/bankform

While we have provided samples of completed bankruptcy forms, you can download and print forms from this site to use as needed when filing your case.

# INDEX

## A

Absentee ownership, 84
Accounting system, 22
Acknowledgment form, 99
Agent, 103
Allowable deductions, 131
American Bankruptcy Institute, 128
Articles of incorporation, 79
Assets:
   attached, 34
   garnished, 34
   keeping, 48–49
   liened, 34
   protecting, 53–54
Attach assets, 56
Attached, bank accounts, 49, 56
Attorneys, bankruptcy, 10–13, 82, 90, 95, 97–98, 107, 110
Auctions, 52
Automatic stay, 15, 64

## B

Bank accounts attached, 34, 49
Bankruptcy:
   basic process, 5
   candidate for, 3–4
   categories, 55–56
   consequences of, 64–65
   decision to file, 1
   filing implications, 70–71
   forms, preparing, 95
   papers online, 95
   petition, 72
   preparing for, 40–41
   trustees, 17, 50, 53
Bankruptcy Act, 82
Bankruptcy clerk, 98, 104, 107, 109
Bankruptcy court, 58
Bankruptcy judges, 17, 66, 109
Bankruptcy law, 17, 41, 53
Bankruptcy petitioner, 112